*

RECOLLECTIONS

AND REFLECTIONS

*

RICHARD STRAUSS

RICHARD STRAUSS

*

RECOLLECTIONS
AND REFLECTIONS

Edited by WILLI SCHUH

*

English translation

by L. J. LAWRENCE

GREENWOOD PRESS, PUBLISHERS
WESTPORT, CONNECTICUT

Library of Congress Cataloging in Publication Data

Strauss, Richard, 1864-1949.
    Recollections and reflections.

    Translation of Betrachtungen und Erinnerungen.
    Reprint of the ed. published by Boosey & Hawkes,
London, New York.
    Bibliography: p.
    1. Strauss, Richard, 1864-1949. 2. Musicians--
Correspondence, reminiscences, etc.
ML410.S93A372 1974   780'.8   74-72
    ISBN 0-8371-7366-3

Originally published in 1953 by Boosey & Hawkes Limited,
London, New York

Reprinted with the permission of Boosey & Hawkes, Inc.

Reprinted by Greenwood Press, Inc.

First Greenwood reprinting 1974
Second Greenwood reprinting 1977

Library of Congress catalog card number 74-72
ISBN 0-8371-7366-3

Printed in the United States of America

EDITOR'S PREFACE

IN the course of more than fifty years Richard Strauss—prompted, in most cases, by some outside stimulus and with no intention of writing 'literature'—published a considerable number of essays, prefaces, open letters and other papers. Taken as a whole, these writings, sporadic as they are, and printed mostly in periodicals inaccessible today, provide such valuable and precise clues to the composer's attitude towards his art, the great masters of music, his own creative work and important problems of musical tradition and practice, that no justification is needed for collecting them. Moreover, Richard Strauss made available for the present volume, which has been brought out at the suggestion of the editor, some of the essays he had written in the course of the last decade, thereby rendering this collection considerably more comprehensive. His reminiscences, hitherto unpublished, are the most important addition.

The task of selecting and collating the material (the essays are printed in chronological order under the various subject headings) —of revising articles previously published, and especially of editing papers not originally intended for publication, was left to the editor, who accepts responsibility for it. The miscellaneous notes at the end, which in many cases do not follow a set course but in which thoughts, experience and reminiscences are loosely strung together, required some revision and sometimes minor alterations of syntax and punctuation, but the editor studiously avoided disturbing certain peculiarities and even somewhat awkward passages, lest the spontaneous and informal character of these writings should be destroyed.

Of the previously published papers, only those which would still seem to be of general interest have been included. Brief statements, démentis, corrections, replies to questionnaires, congratulatory addresses, letters of thanks addressed to individuals and societies, interviews and similar items have mostly been excluded, as has also everything connected with the problem of copyright and with the 'Rosenkavalier' controversy. The lithographed circular letter on the 'Parsifal' copyright controversy (1894), the preface to the revised edition of Berlioz' 'Textbook of Orchestration' (Leipzig, 1905), and the letter printed by Joseph Gregor as preface to his book 'Richard Strauss, der Meister der Oper' (Munich, 1939), have also been omitted, likewise the fragments of an autobiography published by James Huneker in 'Overtones, a Book of Temperaments' (New York, 1904), and reprinted in the periodical 'Die Musik' (Vol. 4, No. 8, Berlin, 1905).

Editor's notes have been limited to a minimum. The bibliography lists first printings only and indicates which papers are printed from the manuscript. The few additions made by the editor are enclosed in square brackets.

WILLI SCHUH.

Zurich, January 1949

TABLE OF CONTENTS

INTRODUCTION TO 'DIE MUSIK'

A Collection of Illustrated Essays

ART is a product of civilisation. It is not its 'calling' to lead a self-sufficient, isolated existence in accordance with 'laws' which are first arbitrarily formulated or designed to meet the needs of the moment and then proclaimed to be 'eternal': its natural calling is to bear witness to the civilisation of an age and of a people.

If we survey the history of literature and of the plastic arts, this interpretation would appear to be perfectly natural. It is, however, more difficult to define the position of music within any given civilisation, because music offers fewer obvious points of comparison with life. Moreover, if we disregard the dead language of the past, accessible only to the antiquarian, and confine ourselves to the living *lingua franca* of today, the fundamental art form of the 'language' of music is of comparatively recent origin. Strictly speaking, the technical perfection of the forms of musical expression and the continuous extension of the vocabulary of music, coupled with the development of the grammatical and stylistic elements of music, which we owe to the genius of our last great masters, have been created by the spade work of a very few centuries. We observe in the history of music, as in the development of the other arts, an evolution from the representation of indefinite or general and typical concepts to the expression of an orbit of ideas which becomes increasingly more definite, individual and intimate. The fact that the inner course of this development is partially hidden under an outward shell of formal elements has enabled certain aesthetic theorists to do some damage for a considerable time—theorists who, unproductive and therefore shortsighted, appreciated only what was superficial and formal, disregarding what was essential or at least giving it only superficial consideration. They taught the dogma of infallible form, the living soul of art was to them a book with seven seals. Persistently shortsighted as they were, they considered themselves qualified time and again to halt a natural development by uttering their proud and dictatorial 'thus far and no further', or to claim for some period the distinction of being the last and fairest flowering of all possible development. History, unperturbed, deals summarily with such reactionary views and turns to other items on the agenda. At any rate we can say today that the error of those who called a more or less playful formalism the essence of music has been overcome. The history of our masters and of their greatest masterpieces has vindicated beyond all doubt direct contact with life and civilisation.

There are in the literature of music a few very welcome documents imbued with this basic idea. But the appreciation of this development as a whole is by no means general. Consistent research pursuing the idea of development is either entirely lacking or its findings are published in highly technical text books on aesthetics which are not readily accessible to the great music loving public.

There would thus seem to be some justification for publishing a number of essays in non-technical language on the essential aspects of music, with a view to giving uniform and clear expression to the idea of development derived from the position of art in a civilisation.

A monograph on Beethoven would appear to be best suited to form the first volume of such a collection, because the appreciation of Beethoven's position with regard to our civilisation may well offer today the largest field of agreement between friend and foe. It may be hoped that more or less general agreement on this interpretation of Beethoven's life and work will form a sure foundation for agreement on greater and more hotly disputed issues of musical aesthetics.

Charlottenburg, December 1st, 1903.

IS THERE AN AVANT-GARDE IN MUSIC?

I HAVE a great aversion to providing some sort of programme for the aesthetic observations and critical essays on music to be published in this weekly (*Der Morgen*).

I dislike programmes as such. To one reader they promise too much. Another they are apt to influence far too much. A third maintains that a programme upsets the functioning of his own imagination. A fourth prefers not thinking at all to following the lines of other people's ideas. A fifth makes some other excuse — in short, programmes are unfashionable. Now I am usually credited with a good nose for sensational matters and, as certain clever contemporaries have long since found out, I spend my day speculating like a kind of musical tailor how best to satisfy next year's fashions; it was for this reason that I first intended to launch the musical part of this periodical without any editorial blessing (which would have been the most modern thing to do), the more so since by doing this, I hoped to indulge my insuperable aversion to literary labour.

The publishers, however, refused to let it go at that. 'If you are prepared to act as editor at all, Mr. Strauss, it is just not good enough for you merely to play the "Spiritus Rector" behind the scenes. You simply must introduce our new periodical *Morgen* with a short but significant statement since you are, after all, the "Leader of the Moderns" and the "Head of the Avant-Garde".'

Now I hate such statements from the bottom of my heart. In spite of one's good intentions, one cannot avoid speaking more or less *pro domo* and my principle is that one should allow actions and works to speak on one's behalf, but not words. The most daring works of artists have never caused as much confusion as the paper proclamations of their adversaries who endeavour to fight against the works with words. I therefore leave such proclamations now and in the future to those who have no desire to lead a life devoid of slogans, or who are deluded enough to believe that they are capable of halting the natural course of progress with dogmatic prohibitions, such as the opponents of futurist music or such Wagnerians as, sinning against the spirit of their master, have become no less petrified than the Mozartians around Franz Lachner, the Mendelssohnians around Carl Reinecke or the Lisztians behind Draeseke.

In short, I refused stubbornly, but those alluring phrases, 'Leader of the Moderns' and 'Head of the Avant-Garde' which are now so studiously and thoughtlessly bruited about, refused to be driven from my mind and I began to meditate in particular upon the 'avant-garde'.

Meditation is always unpleasant, but this time, at any rate, it had the good effect of making me question myself as to whether there was such a thing as an 'avant-garde'. After continued thought, I could only answer this question with a definite no.

When all is said and done, the genuine narrow Wagnerians consisted of an association of like-minded disciples, whose aim it was to explain and propagate the ideas of their master, to remove errors and misunderstandings, to agitate the indifferent section of the public, confirm the judgment of the well-wishers and repudiate that of the opponents. But it was not these partisans who achieved what progress has been made: the finally decisive driving force, which has brought victory to a Richard Wagner, as to all other great original artists, is the multitude of naïvely receptive listeners: always the most reliable means of progress in art. As compared with the fact, demonstrated time and again by history, that a great artist is instinctively recognised by the great public as a natural genius, even if its judgment of details is not at all clear-headed, the machinations of a narrow group of experts whom one might describe as an 'avant-garde' are not of decisive importance. The main thing is the compelling contact between the creative genius and the mass of listeners willing to appreciate progress, who far exceed the limits of any possible 'avant-garde.' We must not allow ourselves to be confused by the fact that this same great public frequently welcomes easily digestible stuff, commonplaces and even banalities, perhaps for a while more enthusiastically, than what is artistically significant, new and in advance of its time. The public, after all, has two souls, but a third is conspicuous by its absence: it appreciates least of all that art which is neither immediately comprehensible nor eminently forceful. This is the reason for the agonies of disappointment suffered by so many serious musicians whom not even their opponents would accuse of being banal, and of whom not even their friends could say that they were capable of captivating the masses.

Carl Maria von Weber once said of the great public, 'The individual is an ass and yet the whole is the voice of God'. And indeed, the soul of this myriad-headed multitude assembled in a concert hall or theatre for the enjoyment of art, will, as a rule, instinctively appraise correctly what it hears provided that busybody critics or professional rivals refrain from inoculating it with preconceived ideas to prejudice its innocence.

Alexander Ritter once told me a good example of the curious confusion wrought in the critical faculties of an audience by external influences.

When, approximately fifty years ago, Franz Liszt first conducted three concerts consisting of his own orchestral works in Dresden, the performance of these symphonic poems, then heard for the first time, and to be so much maligned later, provoked the completely unbiased audience to tremendous enthusiasm. The papers wrote, the morning after, that Liszt was not a composer at all and the very same people who had given free rein to their splendid enthusiasm the night before, grew ashamed of their excitement. None admitted to having applauded and everyone had a thousand reservations after the event.

But whatever is great can only be impeded in its victorious progress for a little while at the most, and can never be finally halted by the men behind the scenes: thus it was that the great public—the Voice of God—enabled even Franz Liszt to conquer malice and stupidity just as its enthusiasm enabled Richard Wagner in 1876 to defeat decisively all his critics, ill-wishers and detractors.

But although there is not, and need not be, such a thing as an 'avant-garde', in the proper meaning of the word, it is necessary to protect the natural sound judgment of the unprejudiced against the onslaught of those who are forever reactionary, and who labour unceasingly out of ignorance, inability, complacency, or self-interest to stifle the public's innate flair for progress.

After 1876 people honestly believed that the enthusiasm of the great public had silenced the hue and cry of the enemy sufficiently to ensure that they would only attempt behind the walls of the conservatoires to instil their venom against the audacious revolutionary into the innocent souls of harmless students of music where the public could not penetrate. People were beginning to hope that everyone in the musical world would, in future, be allowed to work out his own salvation, writing music as he pleased, according to his talent.

This hope proved false.

Professional musicians, anxiously concerned as they are for their own position, artistically impotent, possessing only a certain musical technique culled from some artistic epoch of the past, stubbornly and violently opposed to all expansion of means of expression and artistic form, and critics whose views of art are based on the petrified aesthetics of the past, are once again stirring abroad as a united 'Reactionary Party' endeavouring more than ever to make things difficult for those who wish to go forward.

Now I find it impossible to call a man a reactionary, just because he prefers Beethoven's 'Eroica' to a feeble modern symphonic poem or because he says he would prefer to see the 'Freischütz' twelve times in succession, rather than some worthless modern opera. To this extent, I am a reactionary myself; but the reactionaries I cannot bear are those who demand that Biblical subjects should be taboo because Richard Wagner took his subjects from the Teutonic legends (here I am, of course, speaking *pro domo*), and those who maintain that it is vulgar to use the valve trumpet as a melodic instrument for the sole reason that Beethoven was forced to let his natural trumpets tackle tonic and dominant only. In short, all those who, armed with great tablets of the law, endeavour to say nay, with their *anathema sit*, to everyone who has the ability and the intention to create something new.

It was Richard Wagner who said, 'I should like to give my Siegfried just once before an audience of appreciative listeners assembled from the four corners of the world and then I'd burn the score.' Thank goodness, we say today, that he didn't do it! 'Siegfrieds' are unfortunately so rare that we cannot afford to be prodigal of such precious gifts. But the idea behind this noble intention of the great master, namely that even a perfect work of art should only be considered as one stage in a great organic development, that it should be planted as seed in the souls of our descendants, to inspire and assist in the birth of even higher and more perfect creations, this wonderful idea we will honour, labouring unceasingly in the continuous perfecting of our art, and never forgetting, over and above the love and admiration we owe to the masters of the past who have found perfection, that art is subject to the selfsame laws as ever-changing life.

Not for us, therefore, the application of dogmatic aesthetics to works which should be judged by their own standards; not for us the tablets of the law which have long since been shattered by the great masters; not for us the high priests who dare stand in the path of a vigorous evolution; not for us all those things whose

existence is justified solely by the fact that they existed yesterday. But let us, in this periodical 'Morgen', extend a welcoming
hand and promise protection and assistance to everyone who has
too much respect for the great masters to desecrate and vulgarise
their work by cheap imitation, be it out of complacency, for the
sake of earning a living or to satisfy an ambition which is not, in
the last analysis, born of art.

Welcome to all those who 'strebend sich bemühen' and may
the reactionary party perish!

Fontainebleau, Whitsuntide 1907.

PREFATORY NOTE TO *AUS DEM MUSIKLEBEN DER GEGENWART*. BY LEOPOLD SCHMIDT

INVOKING my Eulenspiegel nature, which, I suppose, I shall have to carry on my fortunately broad back for the rest of my life, the author of this book has asked me to write a few introductory words. At first this seemed to me just as funny as if I were to ask Dr. Leopold Schmidt to write an overture for my opera 'Elektra'. But when I had a closer look at his book, and discovered on how many points our judgments on art differ, I had to confess that Dr. Schmidt had rightly counted on my equability as far as criticism is concerned, and it is, therefore, with pleasure that I satisfy his wish. I can recommend his book as a survey of the musical events of the last ten years to all those readers interested in the changes wrought in the musical tastes of a man well versed in his subject and most certainly conscientious, although perhaps a little timid in his appreciation of new works. It seems to me significant that Dr. Schmidt has not fought shy of confessing in print that his appreciation of the different phenomena has developed and that his attitude to them has, in many cases, changed with the years.

This open confession will appeal to anyone who has himself experienced in his own head the fluctuations to which the evaluation of different periods of civilisation, of the works of art produced in them and, more especially, of all the various stages of musical development is subject.

What do we not demand of the long-suffering critic! I am perfectly ready to confess that a critic has done his duty when he has communicated his momentary impressions in parliamentary form to his readers, provided, of course, that he is equipped with general knowledge of his subject and artistic intuition.

The decision to what extent these momentary impressions may

lay claim to permanence is in any case left to history, which also assesses the merits of the work criticised.

Lest I create the impression of having taken up my pen for the sole purpose of prefacing Schmidt's book with commonplaces, I hasten to explain, at the risk of being thoroughly misunderstood, that critics who do their duty as defined above are not always the most interesting for the artist. To me there is nothing more stimulating that the criticism of a deadly enemy who has listened with the preconceived intention of picking holes in the work wherever possible. The more acute his intelligence the less likely will he be to let pass even the least apparent weaknesses which the enthusiast or even the sympathetic listener is bound consciously or unconsciously to overlook. Since it is the hardest thing in the world for each one of us to become conscious of his own weaknesses, the usefulness of a deadly enemy for the furtherance of self-criticism, provided one practises it at all, is evident.

It is a further platitude that all really great works, no matter how new and unusual their form and content may be, can stand even the most derogatory criticism just as they can dispense with enthusiastic acclamation.

I have frequently smiled to myself when colleagues of mine who are somewhat more sensitive than I am have been highly incensed if the critics' praise of their work failed to come up to their expectations. What a lot of nonsense was written at the time about the damage Hanslick's pamphlets on Wagner were supposed to have wrought.

I am touching here on the interesting relationship between author and critic.

Whereas the minor representatives of the latter profession usually consider it incumbent upon them to preserve intact their sacred critical independence by isolating themselves from the creative artists, the more cultured members of this responsible and much maligned profession have always considered it their duty to gain the necessary insight into the workshop, the ideas and the intentions of the creative artist by constant intercourse with him. How is a critic to judge what an author has achieved if he does not know what was his intention?

If we disregard the critical observations made by creative artists such as Berlioz, Schumann, Liszt and Wagner, normal theoretical criticism is mostly retrospective in character.

Not every work of art is so mature as to give perfect expression to the intentions of its creator. How many poetical and rapt souls have failed to give this final and energetic polish to their work. Should we for this reason disregard masters like Robert Schumann, Brahms, Bruckner and Berlioz as dramatists? Are not their creations, as stages in development, necessary and entrancing?

It is precisely those works which find it difficult to maintain their position between the masterpieces of the first order and trash (those two captivating extremes which are the darlings of the public and the box office), that call for a conscientious evaluation of their importance and for a dogmatic exposition of the noble intentions of their creators, because they are devoid of creative power of such elemental force as to finally defeat all opposition. It does not require much expert knowledge to notice that, apart from magnificent characteristics, these works possess weaknesses which are more easily discernible to the casual observer than their good points, but unfortunately it is in just such works that the superficial critic tries hardest to exhibit his 'understanding'. To illumine sympathetically the beauty of such works (not, as is often done today, by claiming that there is no difference between the euphony of Wagner's and Brahms's orchestra) and to pass over in tactful silence the less successful points until these beauties are known and appreciated, this would in my opinion be a grateful, almost productive task for our critics, in order to introduce the great public gently to works which influence the formation of a refined taste in art.

Above all, there is room for a revision of the works acclaimed in the past, for a detailed examination of the extent to which works can hold their own in our time, lest e.g. a *Martha*, or a *Robert der Teufel* is uncritically allowed to pass merely because our grandmothers liked it, whereas the strictest standards are applied to the most talented productions of our contemporaries, without reflection as to how beneficial it would be for our culture if the place occupied by the unworthy were allotted to good works of art of the second and third rank. Our theatrical culture would be in a better condition if the works of Hermann Goetz, Cornelius, Alexander Ritter, Berlioz, Spohr's *Jessonda*, Weber's *Euryanthe*, not to mention Young Germany, which finds it even more difficult to win a modest position in a German repertoire, were found more frequently on our theatre bills.

Surely it is not a good sign that our repertoires constantly alternate between works like *Tristan* and *Meistersinger* on the one hand and *Mignon* and *Pagliacci* on the other. If our public had been trained and forced to listen to and to appreciate good music, let us say of second class standard, operas like *Fidelio*, *Freischütz*, and *Figaro* would not show an annual decrease in takings nor would the 'Lords, Ladies and Gentlemen' satisfy their artistic urge by listening nightly to the silliest of operettas or to positively inane music hall performances.

These complaints are, of course, as old as the history of music. To emphasise them time and again, at the risk of being tedious, is the duty of anyone who has the interest of our musical life at heart.

I wish to thank the author of this book for having given space at the beginning to this long-standing complaint of the artist.

As for my personal attitude towards criticism, about which the good reader would, presumably, wish to hear something authentic, I wish to say, quite briefly, the following: if my works are good and of any importance for a possible further development of our art, they will maintain their position in spite of all positive opposition on the part of the critics, and in spite of insidious denigration of my artistic intentions. If they are worthless, not even the most gratifying box office success or the most enthusiastic acclamation of the augurs will keep them alive. Let the pulping press devour them, as it has devoured so many before (and as it will do, whether I like it or not)—I shall not shed a tear over their grave. My son will, no doubt, out of filial piety, play my tone poems from the manuscript for a while on the piano with a friend, and then that will end too, and the world will continue on its course.

Garmisch, 20th November, 1908.

OPEN LETTER TO A LORD MAYOR

Your Honour,

Please forgive me if, prompted by interest in your beautiful city [Nuremberg] and its artistic life, I address myself to you.

I conducted an opera there some time ago and would gladly have taken the opportunity of discussing with you the artistic and financial position of the municipal theatre. But unfortunately you were on holiday.

To my regret I must confess that apart from a few excellent guest artists, the artistic level of this performance was so low that I could not help voicing my astonishment.

I now read in the papers that your municipal theatre is passing through a grave crisis.

Would you permit me, your honour, as an expert on theatrical matters with more than thirty years' experience behind me, and as a composer some four or five of whose works have already been performed at your municipal theatre, to give you my opinion on this problem?

You have already contributed so much by your energy to the magnificent development of the community of which you are the head that it would really be deplorable if you failed to apply this energy to the improvement of the artistic status of your city. As I have hinted above, I found in your city an orchestra which, apart from the orchestra in Lemberg in Galicia, was the worst I have ever come across—and I have conducted orchestras in practically the whole of the civilised world. In many very much smaller towns such as Elberfeld, Krefeld, Hagen i.w., Quedlinburg, etc., I have found orchestras of higher quality and greater accomplishment than in your great city. The supporting cast was either mediocre or quite impossible, the chorus in such a state that I cannot imagine works like *Tannhäuser* or *Lohengrin* being given an even remotely satisfactory performance.

It is absolutely out of the question to blame the director of the theatre, whom I know to be an expert on the theatre and a man of ideas: in my opinion the blame rests solely with the system. As far as I know, the theatre has been leased to the director, who is responsible for paying not only an exorbitant rent but all also the salaries, including those of the orchestra and chorus. This is an impossible state of affairs.

If an opera house is to satisfy reasonably moderate artistic requirements it can never show a net profit. The examples one might adduce of municipal theatres-cum-opera houses which were positive gold mines for their directors are irrelevant, because the artistic standards of such theatres were invariably such that they could only be described as music halls.

In my opinion your municipal theatre cost far too much to build. If two million marks had been spent on the erection and establishment of the theatre and the remainder had been used to subsidise its performances, a director would have enough to live on and at the same time could do good work.

But since the worst has happened and this far too expensive theatre has been built, one cannot possibly leave it in its present disgraceful state of artistic disrepair. You will never be able to maintain a municipal theatre in keeping with the size and importance of your city unless the city fathers make up their minds to appoint a permanent orchestra of a definite size, consisting of 14 first and 14 second violins, 14 violas, 8 'cellos, 7 double basses, 4 flutes, 4 oboes, 4 clarinets, 4 bassoons, 8 horns, 4 trumpets, 4 trombones, 1 tuba, 2 harps, kettledrums and percussion, subsidised with a sum of at least 200,000 marks per annum plus pension fund.

Add to this a cash sum of 300,000 marks per annum and your theatre will join the company of the better medium-grade municipal theatres. Any other attempts at improvements will be in vain; no new director, no matter how large his private fortune or extravagant his promises, will succeed in producing anything but a miserable cast and a pitiable orchestra whose performances will not attract the public, nor will the demon of insolvency ever depart from your theatre.

The Royal Opera at Berlin, the Court Opera in Vienna— large theatres both of them, and sold out practically every night —are subsidised to the tune of one million marks, the municipal theatre in Düsseldorf receives an annual subsidy of 500,000 marks; and yet you expect your director to pay rent, put on good performances, and keep the wolf from the door.

Use your influence to change all this, your honour, and let the restoration of this theatre and orchestra become the crowning glory of your great achievements.

Yours respectfully,

DR. RICHARD STRAUSS.

MUNICIPAL REPERTORY THEATRE ASSOCIATION:
A SUGGESTION

IN the year 1849 Richard Wagner wrote a paper entitled: 'Plan for the organisation of a German National Theatre for the Kingdom of Saxony'. Wagner reports that this plan was received with derision by the persons to whom the minister had seen fit to submit it. It has never been carried out and has been hibernating unnoticed these 65 years in the Collected Works. Yet every word of it is so important that no opportunity should be missed of drawing the attention of the public to the invaluable lessons the great master gives to all those who are interested in the development of the German theatre. This essay contains a few of the most important points, selected at random, perhaps thus to stimulate a renewed study of the plan. Under the heading 'branch theatres' Wagner's draft contains observations on the relationship between the municipal theatre in Leipzig and the Royal theatre in Dresden. If we read these remarks attentively we realise that had his plan been carried out there would have been laid the only sure foundation on which the German theatre could flourish. We all know that Wagner turned his back on the German theatre when his ideas on the restoration of the theatre miscarried and that he built his wonderful festival theatre in Bayreuth, which, apart from the Prinzregenten Theater in Munich, is still the only one of its kind. If we survey the evolution of the German stage since 1849, when Richard Wagner observed that none of the other provincial towns had been able to maintain a permanent theatre, no matter how modest, we find not only that every German town with a population of more than 20,000 now maintains a permanent theatre, but that operas are performed there which make the highest possible demands on the artists—performances by an orchestra of between 40 and 50 players and a chorus of 40 with which anyone who has ever witnessed a performance of *Tannhäuser* or *Lohengrin* in one of these small municipal theatres—I am not referring to the small court theatres subsidised by the munificence of noble princes—will be only too painfully familiar.

Today all these theatres are in a more or less critical position. The directors complain that the house is empty and that the competition of the cinema is too strong, whereas the public has been complaining for many years about the poor quality of the performances, that is if it has not stayed away altogether. The financial result of all this can be easily seen. We are inclined to forget how times have changed. In the good old days, when everything was more or less rooted in the soil, the good people of a small town who rarely if ever ventured beyond its walls had no standard of comparison and were therefore more contented with poor performances than they are today when almost everybody travels and even the little man has seen, while on holiday, a performance of *Die Walküre* in Vienna, of *Lohengrin* in Berlin and of *Die Meistersinger* in Munich. I myself have frequently been told on asking educated inhabitants of comparatively small towns whether they ever went to the theatre, 'No, I never go to the theatre here. If I want to hear something worth hearing I go to Dresden or Munich. It only takes two or three hours by a fast train'. It is not after all surprising and should really be considered as a good sign that those who patronise the cheap seats should prefer a relatively good film to a poor performance of *Die Walküre*.

The greatest obstacle to the cultivation of good taste in art and the circumstance which demoralises the public most is poor quality of performance. But how is the director of a small theatre to maintain a high standard if unless he receives subsidies of some kind he must reckon with ever-dwindling resources and is moreover completely at a loss to know how to attract the public anew. In the good old days people imagined that they could continue to attract the public by offering to it as many new works as possible (*cf.* the Pollini régime in Hamburg and the Angelo Neumann régime in Prague). People thought curiosity would be stronger than the disgust engendered by poor performances. This principle has long since failed. After having endured two or three badly produced and therefore ineffective new works, the public refuses to rise to the bait of the fourth. Experience has shown that only those theatres which habitually provide carefully and thoroughly rehearsed performances can count on a steady audience. In Italy and France conditions are better. In Italy five or six operas only are performed in each season, each of which is carefully rehearsed for six weeks. French theatres, on the other hand, never put on a new work without rehearsing it carefully for three months. The director of a small German theatre usually takes pride in producing a new work in the shortest possible time. I myself, when I once had to conduct *Rosenkavalier* at a medium-sized theatre, was told by one such man with a glow of satisfaction that the work had been put on after three orchestral rehearsals in all. The performance went accordingly. Anybody who has had to conduct a *Tristan* 'rehearsed' for a single fortnight or an *Elsa* 'rehearsed' for a week will understand our dilemma.

How are these small theatres to be enabled to put on well-rehearsed performances? Although it may not be possible to put it into practice as it stands, the idea put forward below should be taken as a suggestion which I will gladly withdraw in favour of any plan guaranteeing the possibility of good theatrical performances.

It is obvious that a small town of let us say 35,000 inhabitants (and all these towns nowadays boast a theatrical season offering both plays and operas for six or eight months in the year), even when subsidised by the municipal authorities, cannot possibly afford the expense involved in producing operas which are fairly presentable. The director of course applies the principle mentioned above of letting one new work follow the next. He cannot possibly hope to put on any of the works on the repertoire more than three or four times during the winter, even if it is successful. There is not enough time to rehearse these new works adequately, the quality of the performance is poor and even a public whose demands are moderate and which would gladly accept passable performances stays away. What would therefore enable even these comparatively small theatres to produce well-rehearsed and carefully prepared performances with modest means? This is where I suggest the municipal theatre repertory association. Let us assume that three neighbouring towns form an association, in that each puts at the disposal of the director of a theatre an annual subsidy of 50,000 marks. The director could be expected to work for ten months the first of which, let us say the month of August, would be used for rehearsals. The company would then perform in the first town for three months, September, October, November, thus acquiring a repertoire which could be performed without difficulty and without further rehearsals in the second town during the months of December, January and February. The company would then perform in the third town in March, April and May, and would then go on holiday for two months. In the following year the theatre season in the first town which in the previous year had lasted from September till November, would be changed to December, January and February, and so on for three years. A town of 35,000 inhabitants might well raise a subscription for a three months' season which would allow the director a moderate salary but it cannot guarantee good attendances for six or seven months in the year.

It is not advisable, as has been frequently attempted, to undertake to play in two or three towns on two or three different days, because the strain on the artists is unnecessarily severe and there is insufficient relaxation and continuity of study. The town which enjoys the services of the theatre let us say in September, October and November of one year could postpone all social festivities to the months in which the theatre is not in the town. This arrangement alone would enable the director to conclude contracts for several years, and he would build up slowly a well-rehearsed repertoire, and a well-trained orchestra. Should it really be impossible to find in Germany thirty neighbouring towns prepared to maintain on this basis ten theatres guaranteeing well-presented and carefully rehearsed performances? Should it really be impossible to unite the three Burgomasters of three such neighbouring towns or the three town councils in this effort? I think it will be difficult, and when one sees how two neighbouring towns like Barmen and Elberfeld, which really form only one town, cannot agree on a common theatre it would appear almost impossible. But I cannot resist making this suggestion, because it is only on some such basis that we may expect the theatre to flourish and to raise the aesthetic standards of our nation. There would be an end to the general complaint of financial difficulties on the part of the small theatres and a great service would be rendered to art and the public.

To return in conclusion to the point from which we started, may I be permitted a small epilogue:

The request that Richard Wagner's last will with respect to *Parsifal* be fulfilled has provoked hilarity in the German Reichstag from all parties. The Prussian Chamber of Deputies has recently been discussing the 'exploitation of juvenile shepherds' in the Allgäu and in East Elbia (at which there arose 'homeric laughter'—outside Parliament—from the Vistula to the Lech). But has any of our parliaments ever been known to discuss the exploitation and starvation wages of our brave orchestral musicians and choirs?

Why should not our parliaments for once discuss some such Wagnerian plan for the foundation of a German National

Theatre or, if they would really be forced to confess their ignorance on the subject, why should they not appoint a legislative committee of experts to deal with these serious matters of art? I might even be persuaded to become the second Vice-President of such a parliament of artists. I have no doubt that we artists would come to some agreement with our German princes, well-disposed as they are to artistic endeavours, no less than with our cabinet ministers.

[1914]

OBSERVATIONS ON THE OPERATIC REPERTOIRE

EVER since the days of the late Angelo Neumann or Pollini and other potentates of the German stage, German theatre directors have considered it a point of honour to be able at the end of the season to point to as many new works or new productions as possible which have been 'put on'. There was some justification for this principle in medium-sized towns where it was necessary to solicit the custom of a comparatively limited public by offering one new work after another. This method, however, by no means invariably fulfilled its purpose, as is proved by the fact that these new productions, insufficiently rehearsed and badly staged as they were, succeeded only in exceptional cases, usually had to be withdrawn from the repertoire after two or three performances and thereby provoked amongst the audience a feeling of disappointment so powerful that even so-called first performances ceased to have any attraction. This is sufficient to prove that the ambition to produce the largest possible number or works must not be the decisive factor in the planning of the programme or, in other words, that it is not quantity which matters. It is only the quality of a performance which can attract the public to a theatre in the long run, and which can give the public that implicit faith, which it must have if it is to attend regularly.

The situation has been rendered more complicated since the war and the revolution, in that the presentation of new works and careful new productions of comparatively older works is subject to even greater difficulties than before.

The rapid increase in holidays, the enormous cost of new productions and countless other lesser factors make it necessary to choose very carefully, which means that the largest theatres find it almost impossible to experiment with first performances and untried new works. In my opinion, cities like Berlin and Vienna are quite unsuited to pronounce judgment on untried new works. The fact that the composition of the audience is left entirely to chance and the enormous influence wielded by metropolitan criticism alone would make it appear inadvisable to entrust to the vicissitudes of such a metropolitan first performance a work only too likely to make abnormal demands on receptivity. That is the reason why I, in full agreement with General-Intendant von Hülsen, who was a very experienced man, never put on a first performance in Berlin. Dresden which, under the inspired leadership of Schuch, was in a position to satisfy my artistic requirements as well as Berlin had the advantage that two-thirds of the audience consisted of friends and patrons from elsewhere, and the critics who came to Dresden were in a better frame of mind to appreciate the opera undisturbed.

From all these experiences I conclude that medium-sized and even small theatres, of which there is such a very large number, especially in Germany, are much more suited for first performances than, for example, Vienna and Berlin, provided that their artistic standards are high enough.

If such a work is moderately successful, let us say in Karlsruhe or Stuttgart, the system of subscription which is usual in such theatres will enable the director to keep it on the repertoire, even if it is a financial failure, for long enough to allow the verdict of the first-night audience to be confirmed or corrected. If a new work fails to be an outstanding success in a town like Vienna, the effect of derogatory criticism or of the poor attendance at the second or third performance is so catastrophic and influences other theatres to such an extent that a first performance, unless it is an outstanding success, can completely ruin a work which, had it first been performed in a smaller theatre, might by and by have made more friends and might have conquered more and more stages, to be kept alive for at least some little time.

D'Albert's opera *Tiefland*, which was performed for years by small and medium-sized theatres with increasing success until it became a hit much later at the Berlin State Opera, is an interesting example of this. At least thirty or forty new operas are written in Germany every year. I could present at the most three or four of these in Vienna. Who is to accept the responsibility for perhaps murdering such a work once and for all in the opera at Vienna, no matter how carefully it has been selected?

Exempla loquuntur

When I took over my post in Vienna the ambition to produce a respectable number of new works existed even there.

Thirty years in office proved to me that a new work of any pretentions claims the exclusive attention of orchestra and cast for at least three to four months. The first two years of my stay here in particular showed that the production of new works only a small percentage of which brought moderately lasting success to the Vienna opera handicapped me considerably in the execution of what I considered to be my real artistic task, namely, to effect the greatest possible improvement in the *quality* of the performances and to build up a truly exemplary classical repertoire. This was the reason why I decided, at the end of last year's season, to suggest to my colleague Schalk that we should discontinue to accept new works so long as our present extremely difficult position lasted, until the so-called classical repertoire (in which I would also include all those modern works which have maintained their position on the stage) had been more or less safeguarded, and that in future only those of the more recent operas should be accepted by the Vienna State Opera which had to some degree proved their vitality in the provinces.

For the reasons given above the Vienna State Opera cannot and should not, of this I am convinced, be an experimental institute but rather, as it were, a kind of academy in which a select repertoire is performed in the most exemplary manner possible.

To mention only one example: When I came to Vienna neither *Don Giovanni* nor *Figaro*, nor *Così fan tutte* had become 'established', as they say in the language of the stage. It is therefore my endeavour to improve the quality of a production as far as possible, even if it be a production of Gounod's *Faust*.

In addition to this there are a number of subordinate factors which are by no means unimportant.

The conditions in which an opera house can flourish differ from those in which a theatre flourishes. The former has a definite traditional repertoire, as is shown by the fact that operas of such low quality that they should have vanished long since, for example, *Margarethe*, *Mignon*, *Martha*, *Lucia* or *Der Trompeter von Säckingen*, continue to attract because of their good vocal parts, provided they are sung by good soloists. Opera audiences are moreover far more conservative than theatre audiences. Opera audiences on the whole have no desire to hear new works: ever since *Fidelio* and *Tristan* all good new works have had to be forced upon them. And how many works in the past 150 years have deserved to be thus exhibited? How many operas since *Parsifal* have really proved to be a permanent gain for the German stage? How many of the new works which have since been produced have had twenty-five performances on one and the same stage? How many have had ten, or even two or three performances?

A theatre can easily afford to put on a new play once a fortnight, and to replace it by another after six or ten performances if it has failed. An orchestral society can afford to present to its subscription audience without financial loss a new orchestral work in each concert after three orchestral rehearsals.

But it is plain nonsense to put in motion the enormous machinery of an operatic stage for two or three performances, thus paralysing the whole repertoire for three or four months, in order to rehearse one of these modern pieces, most of which require a great deal of preparation; nor would either the press or the public be gratified by such an undertaking. No responsible director will ever accept the responsibility for such a policy.

In Vienna there is the additional difficulty that our best soloists can be persuaded only with very great pains to learn and sing the usually extremely exhausting and difficult vocal parts of a new opera. And who today would want to, who would be able to 'compel' a Jeritza, a Kurz, a Piccaver? The difficulties of such a new part put all persuasive powers to shame, as I can illustrate with dozens of examples from my own experience as a composer and conductor.

But, and this is typical of Vienna, a new work without 'stars' is foredoomed to failure: the public has no faith in an opera which the leading artists will not touch, and yet the composers who suffer are the first to attack the innocent conductor and to abuse him, especially if, *horribile dictu*, he happens to be writing operas himself.

There are, however, exceptions to every rule and there is an exception to my attitude towards new operas in so far as composers living in Austria, and especially in Vienna, have a right to be heard in the Vienna State Opera, even at the risk of failure. This is the reason why in the course of the last three years new operas by Bittner, Kienzl, Korngold, Schmidt, Schreker, and Weingartner have been performed at the State Opera, and next year there will be added to the list *Der Schatzgräber* by Schreker, *Fredegundis* by Schmidt, *Der Zwerg* by Zemlinsky. In this connection I should like to state that the performance of *Der Schatzgräber* last year was postponed owing to adverse circumstances such as may happen in any theatre, and through no fault of my own.

There is one possible solution for this problem of new operas which is so rational that it will probably not even be put to the test: We have in Vienna the 'Volksoper', an excellent institution which, instead of performing the same repertoire as the State Opera, could be established as a theatre for trial performances of new operas and could be subsidised accordingly, provided that there really are sufficient people interested in hearing a brand new opera every month.

To sum up, I am completely devoid of the (old-fashioned) ambition to produce as large as possible a number of new operas every season. I wish to achieve a high standard of performance. Let objective criticism decide how far I have succeeded in putting my endeavours into practice.

[1922]

TEN GOLDEN RULES

For the Album of a Young Conductor

1. Remember that you are making music not to amuse yourself but to delight your audience.
2. You should not perspire when conducting: only the audience should get warm.
3. Conduct 'Salome', and 'Elektra' as if they were by Mendelssohn: Fairy Music.
4. Never look encouragingly at the brass, except with a short glance to give an important cue.
5. But never let the horns and woodwind out of your sight: if you can hear them at all they are still too strong.
6. If you think that the brass is not blowing hard enough, tone it down another shade or two.
7. It is not enough that you yourself should hear every word the soloist sings—you know it off by heart anyway: the audience must be able to follow without effort. If they do not understand the words they will go to sleep.
8. Always accompany a singer in such a way that he can sing without effort.
9. When you think you have reached the limits of prestissimo, double the pace.*
10. If you follow these rules carefully you will, with your fine gifts and your great accomplishments, always be the darling of your listeners.

(*ca.* 1922)

---

*Today (1948) I should like to amend this as follows: Go twice as slowly (addressed to the conductors of Mozart!)

ON COMPOSING AND CONDUCTING

IT is simply untrue to say that one can compose 'everything', if 'composing' be defined as the translation of a sensual or emotional impression into the symbolic language of music. It is, of course, equally true that one can paint in sounds (especially certain movements), but one always runs the risk of expecting music to do too much and of lapsing into sterile imitation of nature. No matter how much intelligence and technical knowledge go to the making of such music, it will always remain seccond-rate.

I am convinced that the decisive factor in dramatic effect will be a smaller orchestra, which does not drown the human voice as does a large orchestra. Many of our younger composers have already found this out for themselves. The orchestra of the opera of the future is the chamber orchestra which, by painting in the background of the action on the stage with crystalline clearness, can alone realise precisely the intention of the composer with regard to the vocal parts. It is after all an important desideratum that the audience should not only hear sounds but should also be able to follow the words closely.

My conducting, too, has frequently been criticised because, more especially at the beginning, people found fault with the *tempi* of my performances of Beethoven. But I ask, 'Who would today assert dogmatically that Beethoven himself wished a tempo to be taken at a particular pace? Is there such a thing as an authentic tradition in such matters?'

There is no such tradition and that is why I hold that it must be left to the purely subjective artistic acumen of the conductor to decide what is right or wrong. I reproduce every work of Beethoven's, Wagner's, etc. according to my insight into these works, gained in the course of many years, in the conviction that this is the only true and right way.

Time and again I tried to return to the symphonic literature which has absorbed and fascinated me from my youth. But to this day nothing worthwhile would come into my head. Even programme music is only possible and will only be elevated to the sphere of art, if its creator is above all a musician capable of inventing and creating. Otherwise, he is a charlatan, because the quality and cogency of musical invention are the foremost factors even in programme music.

It is perhaps due to the spirit of the age that our successors, our 'younger generation', our 'moderns' can no longer accept my dramatic and symphonic work as a valid expression of the musician and the man in me, which is alive therein, although its musical and artistic problems have as far as I am concerned already been solved at the point at which they begin for 'the younger generation'. We are all children of our own age and can never jump over its shadow.

[1929]

PREFACE TO

EIN ORCHESTERMUSIKER ÜBER DAS DIRIGIEREN :

By HANS DIESTEL

DEAR HERR DIESTEL,

When from 1886 to 1889 I first conducted operas as 'Royal Director of Music' in the Court Theatre at Munich (such things still existed in those days with unlimited subsidies and singers without contractual holidays) my father, who was then 65, still occupied his seat as first hornplayer as he had done for 45 years, always arriving from a fabulous sense of duty one hour before the performance was due to begin, concerned not only lest he should bungle his own difficult solo passages in *Cosí fan tutte*, but also worried lest his inexperienced son at the conductor's rostrum should make a blunder.

It was at this time that he, who had admired Lachner and opposed Bülow, remarked with some irony: 'You conductors who are so proud of your power! When a new man faces the orchestra—from the way he walks up the steps to the rostrum and opens his score—before he even picks up the baton we know whether he is the master or we'.

Using this remark as a motto, as it were, for your book, I would say to my esteemed colleagues: Don't be too proud of your three curtain calls after the third Leonora overture. Down there in the orchestra amongst the first violins, in the back amongst the horns or even at the other end at the timpani there are argus-eyed observers, who note each of your crochets or quavers with critical regard, who groan if you wave your baton furiously in their faces conducting *Tristan* 'alla breves' in four, or when you celebrate the movement 'By the Brook' or the second variation in the adagio movement of the 'Ninth' by beating twelve complete quavers. They even revolt if you constantly shout 'ssh' and 'piano, gentlemen' at them during the performance, whilst your right hand constantly conducts forte. They wink if you say at the beginning of a rehearsal 'the woodwind is out of tune' but cannot indicate which instrument is playing too high or too low. The conductor up there may imagine that they follow reverently each move- ment of his baton, but in reality they go on playing without looking at him when he loses his beat and they blame his 'indi- vidualist interpretation' for every false tempo when he is, let us say, conducting a symphony for the first time which they have played a hundred times before under better conductors.

During one rehearsal when my baton had been mislaid and I was just about to pick up another, the first solo viola player of the Vienna Philharmonic called out to me, 'Not that one, Doctor,— it's got no rhythm'.

In short the stories of how conductors have been caught out by members of the orchestra would fill volumes. And yet this mali- cious mob, who plod their weary way in a chronic *mezzoforte*, who cannot be flattered into accompanying *pp* or into playing chords in a recitative precisely unless the right man happens to be at the rostrum, with what enthusiasm do they not play— tortured though they be by blunderers with no idea of rehearsing, tired out as they are by giving lessons—with what self-sacrifice do they not rehearse if they know that their conductor will not worry them unnecessarily, how readily will they not obey his slightest gesture on the evening of the performance (especially if he has let them off a rehearsal), when his right hand, fully mas- tering the high art of conducting conveys to them his exact in- tentions; when his eye surveys their playing severely yet benevo- lently, when his left hand does not form a fist in *ff* passages and does not unnecessarily restrain them in *p* passages.

My dear Herr Diestel! For twenty years you played under me in the Royal Berlin Orchestra at a time when I had really learned how to conduct and when I had an opportunity of improving my technique every morning at the head of a first-class orchestra and of proving my worth every night. The idea that your meritorious book is the result of our common artistic labours flatters me.

What is new about your book as against Richard Wagner's monumental volume *Uber das Dirigieren* is the fact that here for the first time the activity of the conductor is examined as seen from the orchestra pit, i.e. from below, and not from outside or from the conductor's rostrum. Every objective reader will have to admit that your book examines exhaustively with scientific accuracy and fundamental knowledge a subject which has so far been treated mostly with professional aridity or frivolous super-ficiality.

The only wish with which I would therefore launch this book is that it may be read sedulously. It will profit more particularly those of my conductor colleagues who, modestly taking their place behind the composer, are seriously interested in ensuring that orchestral music should once again be heard with the ears instead of with the eyes.

Yours sincerely,

DR. RICHARD STRAUSS

Verenahof, Baden b. Zürich, 15th July, 1931.

ON CONDUCTING CLASSICAL MASTERPIECES

IT is decisive for the technique of conducting that the shorter the movements of the arm, and the more confined to the wrist, then the more precise is the execution. If the arm is allowed to be involved in conducting—which results in a kind of lever-action the effects of which are incalculable—the orchestra is apt to be paralysed and misdirected, unless it is determined from the start (and this is frequently the case with conductors whose down-beat is imprecise) to play according to its own judgment in tacit agreement as it were, without paying too much attention to the antics of the conductor.

*   *   *

The left hand has nothing to do with conducting. Its proper place is the waistcoat pocket from which it should only emerge to restrain or to make some minor gesture for which in any case a scarcely perceptible glance would suffice.

It is better to conduct with the ear instead of with the arm: the rest follows automatically.

*   *   *

In 50 years of practice I have discovered how unimportant it is to mark each crochet or quaver. What is decisive is that the up-beat which contains the whole of the tempo which follows should be rhythmically exact and that the down-beat should be extremely precise. The second half of the bar is immaterial. I frequently conduct it like an *alla breve*.

It was Richard Wagner who demanded that conductors should grasp the fundamental tempo correctly, since this is all-important for the proper performance of a piece of music; especially in slow movements, he said, distinct bowing of, let us say, a melodic phrase consisting of eight bars was essential. A conductor who interprets aright the *adagio* theme of Beethoven's Fourth Symphony will never allow himself to be led by the rhythmical figure accompanying the first bar into chopping this fine melody up into quavers. Always conduct periods, never scan bars.

At a music festival in the Rhineland 80 years ago Franz Liszt, when conducting the last movement of Schubert's C Major symphony, adapted his beat to the period, i.e. he only used a downbeat once in every four bars. The poor orchestra, unused as it was to the ways of genius, was at a loss how to squeeze in its triplets and concluded that this was no conductor. Second-rate conductors are frequently inclined to pay too much attention to the elaboration of rhythmic detail, thus overlooking the proper impressive rendering of the phrase as a whole and the insinuating lilt of the melody as a whole, which should always be grasped by the listener as a uniform structure.   Any modification of tempo made necessary by the character of a phrase should be carried out imperceptibly so that the unity of tempo remains intact.

We have no authentic metronome figures for the works of our classical masters. Only our music critics seem to have received authentic information on this point straight from the Elysian Fields.

It is probable that the pulse of the present generation beats faster than it did in the age of the post-chaise. This is proved by the fact that the younger generation of today and the Latin peoples rebel against Richard Wagner's 'longueurs', obviously incapable of making themselves at home in the emotional and spiritual atmosphere of an earlier age.

*   *   *

Richard Wagner once wrote that Mozart's allegros 'should be played as fast as possible'. Quite, but not *twice as fast* as possible. The Figaro overture, the two great finales, *Così fan tutte*, Act 1, *Figaro*, Act 2, are usually played far too fast.

The following tempi should not be exceeded:

Così fan tutte finale: metr.   ♩=**136**   (D-major)
Figaro finale: metr.   ♩=**128**   (E-flat major)

Let us not forget that Wagner, with his 'longueurs', could not in 1850 in his worst delirium have meant 'as fast as possible' to denote the insane tempi we hear today. That good old conductor Franz Lachner, whom it is a little unfair to remember as a pedant, once remarked quite correctly to my father: 'In fast movements, when conductor and orchestra have become all too excited, the conductor's art consists in guessing with accuracy the point at which the mad rush can be stopped either by gradual slowing down to the *tempo primo* or even by a well-motivated sudden retardation'. There is such a moment in the D-major passage in the finale of *Così fan tutte*. There must be a restrained entry of the dominant after the two sustained notes. I myself have known so-called geniuses of the baton to rush headlong into these Beethoven and Mozart finales as if their horse had shied and was pulling the reins. I would also mention in connection with this the finale of Beethoven's B flat major symphony which is always played far too fast and should be a comfortable allegretto: *Heiter* does not mean a speed record!

*   *   *

Just before exciting moments or dramatic outbursts (second movement of the Fourth and Fifth Symphonies) Beethoven frequently interposes almost playful 'pianoforte passages', as a man might mechanically and apparently apathetically tap the table with his fingers at times of high nervous tension. These passages should accordingly be played quite loosely, thus the final cadence in the adagio of the B flat major symphony.

The slackening of pace just before a great fortissimo is, for all its popularity, quite unbearable. This is just as amateurish as the drawing out of loud brass passages (e.g. the E-flat major in the

Funeral March of *Götterdämmerung*) or the energetic up-beats. Subjects which the composer himself has drawn out should not be drawn out further (e.g. the woodwind passage in the Third Leonora overture just before the prestissimo). Dreadful also in the wonderful overtures by C. M. v. Weber are the ritardandi in the bars leading to the second subject—especially abominable is the sentimental slowing-down of the 'cello passage in the *Euryanthe* overture, and the cheap ritardando

in that vivacious melody

and especially of the subsidiary subject in A-major of the *Oberon* overture which offends entirely against the style of these virtuoso pieces.

The *Tannhäuser* overture usually offers an example of the false broadening of coda phrases. Keep up the presto to the end without any slowing-down. This also applies to the overture of *The Flying Dutchman*. There must be no slowing down in the trombones before the last *meno mosso* which must be strictly in tempo without ritardando (and not too slowly at that).

MOZART

In Mozart we must distinguish between (usually fast) pieces which present a lively pattern of sound—in these the *cantabile* subsidiary subject should generally be taken a little more quietly (*Figaro* overture, first movement of the G minor symphony)—and (usually slow) movements in which the play of the emotions is frequently carried to heights of passion, e.g. the *andante* of the *Sinfonia Concertante* for violin and viola, a passage which can only be achieved (like so many of Mozart's slow movements) with extremes of rubato. With the exception of Beethoven there is hardly a composer whose tempi are more mistreated or who requires so much delicacy in this respect.

Special rules: *Andante* or *Adagio* 𝄴 to be carefully observed : Introduction of *Don Giovanni* overture, *Andante con moto*, a fairly lively tempo: Cherubino's second aria. No change in tempo in the second half of Zerlina's two arias, above all no allegro, the first half therefore to be taken comparatively fast. This applies also to the duet 'Reich mir die Hand, mein Leben'. The slow movements of the last three great symphonies (G minor, E flat major, C major) should be interpreted and if possible conducted in four; I usually slow down in the last concluding passage (as also in the andante of Schubert's great C major symphony and in Beethoven's first symphony). In some very quick movements it is advisable to stress continuity and to slow down a little at the end. The final fugue of the *Jupiter* symphony and the finale of Brahms's second symphony are cases in question. Mozart's final fugue belongs to the category of movements which Wagner wished to be taken 'as fast as possible': at the beginning of the second part after the development and at the beginning of the third part I retard strongly. In order to allow the fugue to retain a distinct shape at *presto* speed it is necessary to reduce the volume of brass and timpani, and these reductions should be clearly marked in the score. Mahler made the first violins in the first *Figaro* duet play staccato. I made them play cantando, half legato.

During a rehearsal of *Il Seraglio* in the 'nineties in the Munich Residenztheater, Cosima Wagner said to me, 'Your first violins don't sing enough'. In Mozart and in his symphonic opera orchestra the first violins should always 'lead' and should never be allowed to lapse into an inexpressive 'accompanying piano', which in Mozart is usually mistaken for 'orchestral discretion'. Almost invariably in performances of Mozart's operas the sustained middle parts of the woodwind and the high horns in A and G are too loud, thus drowning the quick parlando of the singers. It is therefore impossible to mark too many *pianissimos* in these woodwind parts, which should moreover be observed. The symphonic texture of the string quartet must not be obscured or bungled, since the singer must not only be accompanied but also supported. Mozart writes *ff* on rare occasions only, and only on very rare occasions should his *f* be treated roughly. Beauty of sound is the most important factor here. In Haydn's and Mozart's symphonic works the *forte* passages are subconsciously conceived as *tutti* in the manner of the *concerti grossi*, in which the passages played piano by the solo instruments alternate almost automatically with *forte* passages repeated by the whole orchestra.

In Mozart and Haydn these *forte-tutti* are, as it were, architectonic pillars framing emotional passages, the *fortes* with their natural trumpets, horns and timpani are therefore more the expression of a heightened enjoyment of life than are Beethoven's, whose trumpet octaves and timpani *sforzatos* represent explosions of wildest despair and of defiant energy, only rarely mitigated by the use of the darker and softer trombone. The trumpets, horns, and timpani in the Commendatore's scene in *Don Giovanni* are Beethovenesque; this is far more incisive without trombones which should not therefore be used in this scene. One should also differentiate carefully between *sfz* in Mozart and in Beethoven, and between *sfz* in a *piano* and in a *forte* passage.

* * *

Producers of opera usually make the mistake nowadays of translating each particular orchestral phrase into terms of a movement on the stage. In this matter one should proceed with a maximum of caution and good taste. There is no objection to bringing life into the production by changes of position and new nuances of acting during repetitive passages of music, especially in arias. Preludes of one or two bars frequently, and especially in Mozart, clearly express some gesture on the stage. But each trill on the flute does not represent a wink of the prima donna, nor every delayed chord on the strings a step or a gesture. Whole passages, especially in the finales, are pure concert music and are best left undisturbed by 'play-acting'.

But the worst thing of all is if in *The Magic Flute* the sets are made to clash stylistically with the work especially by the use of lavishly modernised décor. Such new décor, properly speaking, would involve rewriting the libretto in the 'modern' style and re-orchestrating in the style of the *Götterdämmerung*.

*   *   *

HANS VON BÜLOW AS AN INTERPRETER OF
BEETHOVEN

The exactitude of his phrasing, his intellectual penetration of the score combined with almost pedantic observation of the latter, his analyses of the period structure and above all, his understanding of the psychological content of Beethoven symphonies and of Wagner's preludes in particular have been a shining example to me to this day, although I myself have at times modified his incisive dissection of some movements—e.g. of the first movement of the *Eroica*—and although I endeavour to achieve a greater uniformity of tempo. I found particularly memorable the rigid slow temp he used in the *Coriolan* overture, the slow beginning of various scherzi (*Eroica*: bridge passage leading to the funeral march; Ninth symphony: the great working up to the *fortissimo furioso*). Thus he took the three repetitions of the scherzo of the 7th Symphony a little faster each time, not reaching full *prestissimo* until the third time. He started the finale of the A major symphony like a peasants' dance with minor modifications, but took the coda as a tremendously exciting *stretta*.

The only thing he did not correct was the tempo of the *Egmont* overture, which should not be faster than the first movement of the *Eroica*, if only to judge by the indications of speed. It was left to me to bring out the mood of depression and obstinacy implicit in this tragic piece. The wrong tempo would seem to have originated with Mendelssohn. The decisive factor for the fundamental tempo is the second subject of staccato crotchets which Bülow recognised correctly but played too slowly as compared with the first subject (contrast between Klärchen's tragic fate and Egmont's levity). This is immediately followed in the A flat major development by the Klärchen episode.

*   *   *

In the sixth volume of his letters, page 54, Bülow mentions that Wagner had conducted the *presto* of the third Leonora overture *poco a poco accelerando*—'lest the *presto* rush too impetuously into the climax'—I consider to be better, stronger, and more Beethovenesque, and maintain that the whole passage is built on the C major tonic and not the dominant. Nor should it ever degenerate into a mad rush. I effect the real final *accelerando* only four bars before the *ff*. In the whole passage it would be important to stress clearly the rising scale of the respective lowest notes. This is therefore to be rehearsed as carefully as possible.

*   *   *

TWO OVERTURES

Freischütz. I do not agree with Richard Wagner that the great final C major of triumphant innocence should be played entirely piano; this is too much against Weber's intention. But Wagner is quite right; the *fortissimo* brass is too brutal for this beautiful poetical melody. For this reason I make the strings play their melody *forte*, all the brass accompanying piano and only when I come to the high A do I let the strings play *fortissimo* and the brass *forte*.

Third Leonora: people constantly overlook the fact that the transition in the first *allegro* passage to the E major cadence should

be kept *piano* for four bars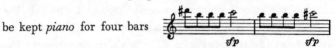

until *forte* is really marked in the score. It is a bad mistake to slow down the last bar in the development before

the entry of the trumpet on the stage.

On the contrary, this whole passage is to be played *accelerando*: after all, Pizarro, as he rushes at Leonore, knows nothing of the B flat of the trumpet. It is further a serious blunder to allow the whole of the woodwind passage before the last *presto* to slow down. If the composer himself draws a theme out the conductor should not slow it down further. Bülow and I maintain throughout the full tempo of hopeful expectation. I am inclined, if anything, to accelerate so that the violin passage enters in the main tempo—not as a mad rush—and only accelerates four bars before the *fortissimo*. Above all, the melodic line must be brought out with the greatest clarity. These things should be obvious to anybody who can read a score—but what is obvious nowadays?

Die Meistersinger: Ever since it has been dubbed 'opera comedy' after the Wagnerian 'longueurs' of the other operas, people have taken to conducting this wonderful work like an operetta, doing the greatest possible violence to the style of the opera. Alexander Ritter once explained to me that each act of a Wagner opera has a uniform symphonic tempo, violent divergencies from which are admissible only in rare (dramatically motivated) exceptions. Thus the score of *Die Meistersinger* stresses the uniformity of the fundamental tempo practically every time a new tempo is introduced by means of signs like $\textbf{♩} = \textbf{♩}$ of previous tempo, and correlates the various parts clearly one to another.

Metr. $♩ = \textbf{56-60}$: The main tempo indication especially of *Die Meistersinger*: very moderate—moderate, moderately fast— characterises exactly the fundamental note: Cultured bourgeois comfort and contentment, fundamental decency, Hans Sach stowering above it all—superiority involves restraint!—interrupted only by the passionate utterances of the lovers and the malicious outbursts of Beckmesser. But even these must be brought into some sort of connection with the fundamental tone of the opera and must never be allowed to assume the proportions of Tristan's passion.

Overture: Very moderate *allegro*, a slight modification in the last bar before the entry of the flute—but the whole of this small episode should be kept within the character of the fundamental tempo and should not be allowed to relapse into an *adagio* and into endless *ritardandi* before the violin passage. The centre movement in E major has the following legend: Main tempo as in the passionate whispers of the love duet. Even the Beckmesser episode (E flat major) is inscribed 'Mässiges Hauptzeitmass'. Beware of taking the chorale which follows too slowly. The scene between Evchen and Walter should be taken with minor modifications to suit the words. It is usually taken far too fast so that the hurried dialogue becomes obscure.

The ensemble passage of the masters, 'Das heisst ein Wort', is inscribed *Vivace ma non troppo*, otherwise the tempo must be slowed down too much when Pogner speaks. Walter's 'Am stillen Herd' is usually started too slowly. The little *ritardandi* and sustained notes prescribed are sufficiently restraining. Not until Sachs's reply, 'Halt Meister', should there be a noble restraint showing intellectual superiority. This passage should not be taken too fluently nor should the intonation be too strong. The following are dreadful nuances: Pogner's indignant 'Dass nur auf

SCHACHER und Geld' and Sachs' sentimentally stupid '*ARME* Poeterei'. Simple, oh so simple! Second act beginning 6/8 and following therefrom 2/4 conversation between David and Magdalene usually too fast and hurried. Likewise the conversation between Pogner and Eva 2/4: moderate and then very leisurely —this is usually taken too fast.

The Cobbler's songs are also usually taken a little too fast, with too little character. Possibly the same tempo as in the overture: Wagner's 'Andante' 'alla breve'. At the end of the second act the bad mistake is frequently made of letting Beckmesser get faster and faster, starting from the moment at which he sings without interruption so that when the fisticuffs start it is impossible to implement the 'a little faster' and the whole scene becomes complete chaos. From the beginning ('Darf ich mich Meister nennen') Beckmesser must maintain the same uncompromising pace.

It is also a mistake to begin Pogner's B flat major 'Will einer Seltnes wagen' as an *adagio* aria. Nor should there be any trace of *adagio* mood about Sachs' lilac monologue and no unnecessary drawing out of

which is after all right from the beginning an impetuous motif going through the head of a worried, meditative Sachs.   Our conductors are always inclined to conduct in accordance with the musical phrase as such, instead of in accordance with its dramatic emotional content. (*Cf.* in this connection the E flat major passage in my own *Elektra*, which is always sung as a mellifluous *cantilena* instead of being sung in highest excitement after the tremendous experience of recognition). If the audience is bored with Wagner, it is the conductors who are to blame: they lack the wider view of the dramatic line of a Wagner act and are unaware that it must be sustained until the curtain drops.

The prelude of Act III is inscribed *moderately* drawn out—it is often played like a true *adagio*.

First act Beckmesser's 6/8 'Ei! Was kümmert doch Meister Sachsen' in the tempo of the first prelude: Metr. 116–128.

Tristan: Cosima Wagner once said—quite rightly—that in *Tristan* the actor's gesture always occurred exactly one bar before the word, and that this had been followed out faithfully in the orchestra and constituted a special *Tristan* style: 'Wohin Mutter' —'Zerschlag es, dies trotzige Schiff'—'Wie lachend sie mir Lieder singen', etc.

*   *   *

After a production of *Parsifal* (Summer 1933): When studying the score with the orchestra I particularly noticed the *ritardandi* which have become traditional: thus in the first subject of the prelude, whose wonderful perfect rhythmic form is positively destroyed when it is played with a sentimental *ritardando*. It becomes unbearable unless it is played with metronomic exactitude, with liturgical 'indifference'. When conducting *Parsifal* one should distinguish between three clearly defined groups of expression, whose style and content must determine the tempo:

The liturgy: This applies especially to

to be sung without sentimental *ritardandi* with sistine 'objectivity': the purely ecclesiastical element.

The narrative group: personified in Gurnemanz who, as a kind of 'evangelist', should be maintained throughout in an objective instructive manner. In his part we find the words which are otherwise very unusual in Wagner: 'Do not drag'. It demands much tact and dramatic intuition on the part of the conductor not to impede the steady flow of music in this part.

The immediate experience (Amfortas, Kundry, Parsifal): This allows free play to a purely emotional presentation to achieve the most immediate effect, provided always that the greatest rhythmical exactitude of declamation is not impaired.

* * *

Conducting is, after all, a difficult business—one has to be seventy years of age to realise this fully!

ON THE PRODUCTION OF 'TANNHÄUSER' IN BAYREUTH

Dear Sir,

In connection with the many important communications you have received arising from the impressions gained in last year's festival, I wish to take the liberty, at the risk of appearing immodest, of sending you these my observations which may be of interest to you for the sole reason that they were written by an orchestral conductor, i.e. by a member of a profession which, owing to its musical limitations, has shown itself to be less capable than the cultured lay public of appreciating the essence of what our great master endeavoured to achieve by creating Bayreuth, because the majority of its members are so score-bound that they are unable to see the drama for the notes.

Amongst the flood of nonsense I had to hear or read last summer concerning the festival in general and the incomparable performance of *Tannhäuser* in particular originating from people who always knew better but invariably failed to do better or at least to make really concrete suggestions as to how one could do better, I noticed particularly that the professional critics, having duly shown that *Tannhäuser* was no drama and should therefore be performed in accordance with the 'laws' of opera, almost unanimously admitted that the playing of the festival orchestra had been of a very high order. It is of course extremely nice of these gentlemen to find something complimentary to say about the Bayreuth *Tannhäuser*, but even this compliment loses in importance if we remember that these same critics are in the habit of concluding their reports on performances at their local theatres of operas such as *Asrael* in Dresden, *Manon* in Vienna, *Cavalleria* in Berlin, *Rose von Strassburg* in Munich, etc., with the words: 'Chorus and orchestra under the practised and careful guidance of our (at times inspired) Mr. X were excellent.' But excellent, after all, means excellent and nothing else, and I have been unable so far to find in any German dictionary an indication that there are degrees of 'excellence'. This is rather unfortunate.

In defence of the critics I can only assume that this indifferent use of the word 'excellent' constitutes nothing more than looseness of style, since I do not imagine for a moment that these critics would wish to compare the performances of their local orchestras with those in Bayreuth. If we assume that the performance of the orchestras in the above-mentioned theatres was characterised by the epithet 'excellent' because their playing did in fact excel the performance on the stage, we should in this particular case have to examine in what respect the instrumental presentation of the *Tannhäuser* score in the festival theatre excelled the orchestral performances mentioned above, i.e., the stylistically perfect realisation of the master's intentions.

To Richard Wagner the highest problem of the opera was the achievement of balance between its dramatic and musical tendencies, and this balance he called 'style'. If I may be allowed to apply the word tendency to the performance of an opera it would seem a condition precedent for a stylistically accurate performance, let us say, of *Tannhäuser* that there should be such a thing as a dramatic tendency and a musical tendency—and that the two should agree. Now it is extremely difficult, if not impossible, for an orchestral conductor at one of our opera houses to achieve balance between his musical tendency and the dramatic tendency, because in my experience the latter is hardly ever in evidence, except in festival performances. Unconcerned by dramatic exigencies one goes on conducting merrily as though nothing had ever existed except subscription concerts in the Gewandhaus at Leipzig, and the poor actors on the stage are promptly demoted to mere singers. The wonderful production of the *scenic and dramaturgical part* in the performance of *Tann-*

häuser in *Bayreuth* in 1891, on the other hand, succeeded for the first time in giving full expression to the poetic and dramatic content of this magnificent work of art, thereby making it a deeply moving experience. But this was the *basis* without which a *correct* execution of the musical element, and not least of the orchestral part, would have been *impossible*.

Let me illustrate this by means of a few examples. In the seventh volume of his collected works, Wagner calls an opera in which the dramatic tendency is at no point allowed to become clearly defined 'a chaos of the most confusing kind', precisely because so many artistic media are used. 'A purely musical effect', he says, 'is made impossible if the dramatic action is left obscure'. What unprejudiced spectator has not himself heard the musical effect of the Bacchanale of the Paris version when played in one of our larger opera houses, as an extremely unpleasant, and violent noise. All that was to be seen was an orchestra struggling in vain with figuring designed for a far more moderate tempo, and in its midst 'one of the sergeant-majors of the baton' (Taktprofessen) (as Lizst once called us) radiating *fortissimo* glory, whilst the puppets up there on the stage performed their ancient, outmoded, indifferent ballet steps without rhyme or reason, a performance not inclined to attract the attention of the most naive of patrons nowadays. In short, this scene did not achieve the slightest effect. This, on the other hand, had to be explained by the critic. It did not occur to anybody to point to the real cause of the trouble, namely that the stage presentation was not in agreement with the author's intention, or rather, that not a single one of the author's intentions had been carried out; but the composer of *Lohengrin*, *Tristan*, *Meistersinger*, could not very well be accused of having made a complete mess of the *musical* revision of the first scene of *Tannhäuser*. What was to be done? A gentleman who had been particularly good at looking up dictionaries ever since his days at the Berlin Conservatoire at last found a wonderful slogan- 'Stylistic difference'. In other words: the music of the new Venusberg scene, being 'Tristanesque', differed stylistically from that of the old *Tannhäuser*. Note that this applied *only to the music!* No bumpkin has so far had the audacity to claim that the poetic and dramatic content of the Bacchanale and of the following scene between Venus and Tannhäuser is out of keeping with the text of the old *Tannhäuser*. But since it may be presumed that nobody will argue that in what is still the only first scene of *Tannhäuser*, poet and musician (forgive the tautology) are for once out of step, or that the means of expression used by the 'musician' are in-adequate to express the poetic idea, and considering that the re-vision of the text of the first scene is in complete stylistic agree-ment with the old *Tannhäuser* text, we are forced to conclude that the music of the first scene would agree in the same way with the music of the rest of *Tannhäuser* if only the performance were right, i.e. stylistically accurate, and if the dramatic inten-tions of the author were clearly realised on the stage, so that the conductor of the orchestra were suddenly to find himself in a position to achieve agreement with these dramatic intentions.

How incomparably beautiful was the effect of the Bacchanale in Bayreuth!

In that performance there was complete agreement between the living gesture, embodied in a dance of formal Greek beauty, and its moving expression in the language of the modern orches-tra, an agreement which constituted a stylistic achievement of the first order. The spectator was justified in saying of this first scene of *Tannhäuser* in the Bayreuth performance: this is *the* Venusberg and I have seen a true picture of Hellenic *joie de vivre*. In this scene, as at the end of the first and during the second act, where he found himself in the chivalrous atmosphere of the medieval cult of the Virgin, and again at the beginning of the third act when he was deeply moved by the noblest ex-pression we have of the mystic expectancy of Christianity, eye, ear and heart alike were fascinated by the glorious impression of a wonderful dramatic poem, fully brought to life by a performance in which all the means of expression used by the author— sculpture, painting, poetry and music—were equally matched. All 'stylistic differences' were suddenly dispelled like 'eitler Staub der Sonne'; let who will dare to assert after this that the Venusberg is out of place in Wagner's *Tannhäuser*.

The measured beauty of the ancient dance as manifested in Bayreuth naturally induced the orchestra to adopt a slower pace than usual, so that the rhythms of the dance (in the ideal sense) played by the orchestra were imbued with the full significance required by the events on the stage, thus automatically necessitating correct presentation. The master says: 'The choice and designation of the right tempo, which allows us to determine immediately whether the conductor has understood the piece, enables good musicians, once they are familiar with the music, to find automatically the right way of playing it because the former involves the conductor's recognition of the latter'.* This means that the right tempo is the decisive factor in a good performance which corresponds to the composer's intentions. Now, leaving aside for the moment the quality and quantity of orchestra and cast, the training of the orchestra, the individuality of the conductor, his lively or quiet manner, his sense of rhythm, etc., the following factors in the drama have a considerable effect on the tempo (and the performance) of the orchestra.

1—*The singer's delivery*; his temperament, his vocal talent, his feeling for significant declamation, his comparative ability to accentuate sharply.

---

*In connection with the tempo problem I would also refer readers to the master's observations on 'Dragging and Rushing' concerning the entirely different manner in which a moderate tempo must be played as against a tempo which is too fast.

Cf. Vol. 8 of the collected works, pp. 349 and 350.

Thus *the moderate tempo of the chivalrous song to Venus*, which I heard *delivered correctly* for the first time by the singer who played Tannhäuser in Bayreuth, is of such decisive importance for the tempo of the overture that the whole of the B major central scene of the allegro passage of the overture, if played at this speed, appears to be *badly orchestrated*, because the figuring in the viola and 'cello parts can no longer be carried out so that, as I have often found in other performances of the *Tannhäuser* overture, the melody and bass only and not the middle parts can be heard. Furthermore, the right tempo and delivery in Elisabeth's prayer, 'Ich fleh' für ihn', are of the utmost importance for the prelude to Act III and those of her aria in Act II for the prelude to Act II.

2—*The singer's ability to act*, to express realistically on the stage the gestures described by the orchestra—and even *Tannhäuser* contains far more of these than one could have imagined before the Bayreuth performance. In connection with this point I should like to draw attention to the dramatic and musical delivery of the orchestral prelude; to the three songs of Tannhäuser to Venus, to Tannhäuser's 'Den Gott der Liebe sollst Du preisen' in the duet of the second act; I would remind you of the wonderful co-ordination of gesture and its musical expression before the words of Venus, 'Wie hätt ich das erworben'; before Elisabeth's, 'So stehet auf' and 'Verzeiht wenn ich nicht weiss was ich beginne', before the Landgraf's words 'Dich treff ich hier in dieser Halle', and 'So sei's! Was der Gesang so wunderbares'.

All these moments and many others, such as the Landgraf's action before the words 'Ein furchtbares Verbrechen ward begangen', made an indescribable impression in Bayreuth *because of the exactitude of dramatic execution and the co-ordination between orchestra and stage.*

I do not suppose that any of the spectators who followed the dramatic development attentively noticed while watching the incredibly gentle movement amongst the troubadours in the firts act just before Wolfram's song: 'Als du in kühnem Sange uns bestrittest', how much the conductor had slackened the pace of the short orchestral ritornello, or how the great breadth of orchestral playing during Elisabeth's miming in Act III seemed natural because the singer who played the part of Elisabeth was able to carry out her movements in an atmospheer of dignified calm in agreement with the orchestra.

3—*Size of the stage*: in the pilgrims' chorus, for example (the pilgrims, by the way, should *remain in motion* and should *not*, as is usual in 'cleverly' directed theatres, go down on their knees before the statue of the virgin which detracts attention from the main action) and in Elisabeth's exit in the third act.

4—*Dramatic and musical training of the chorus*, and size of the chorus. In connection with this I would remind you of the wonderful diction and rhythmic perfection of the welcoming chorus of Act II, which enabled the conductor to attain the right tempo and playing of the march without the chorus which precedes it; further of the excellently enunciated pilgrims' chorus in the third act which (according to Wagner's own words, Vol. 5 of the collected works, page 142) is so important for the phrasing of the first few bars of the overture; finally of the 'enthusiastic rising' of the whole assembly of knights (end of Act II) at 'Mit ihnen sollst Du wallen', after the Landgraf's words to Tannhäuser pointing the way to salvation. The dramatic realisation of this incident as achieved in Bayreuth alone justifies Mottl's considerable increase in pace at this point.

I should like to mention, as an interesting exception, the considerably slower tempo of the prelude to Act III (metr. crotchet $=50$) as compared with the tempo of Tannhäuser's narration (crotchet$=60$). The explanation of this is to be found in the *epic character of the latter*, in contrast to the actual event which the prelude, marked by the master himself 'Tannhäuser's pilgrim-age', is meant to describe.

The examples mentioned above show how difficult it is to play the purely instrumental symphonic parts of the *Tannhäuser* score. In the *Tannhäuser* overture, and the preludes to the second and third acts, the conductor is faced as in none of the later works with the task of uniting a number of elements often dia-metrically opposed by the composer into a symphonic whole. As I have already indicated above, the *events on the stage* pre-determine in the overture the tempo and delivery of the pilgrims' chorus, of the Bacchanalia, of the song to Venus and latter's song to Tannhäuser: 'Geliebter, komm'. As for the prelude to the second act, the fundamental tempo of which is determined by the aria of Elisabeth, the deciding factors are, apart from the sub-jects of this aria, the radiant motif from the finale of Act I announcing Tannhäuser's arrival and the curse of Venus: 'Suche Dein Heil und finde es nie', immediately following on the pert violin passage which I imagine expresses the jubilant spirit of the hunt ('Die Erde hat ihn wieder'); similarly, for the prelude to Act III, it is the motifs of the pilgrims' choruses, of Elisabeth im-ploring and dying a sacrificial death in part immediately con-trasted with the Pope theme, the Pope's curse and the motifs of the repentant Tannhäuser which are all-important. Only a con-ductor of genius like Felix Mottl could *succeed in bringing out these sharp contrasts with the clarity postulated by the action on the stage and in welding them into complete unity by the artistry of his transitions and the restrained modifications of his tempo.* He was assisted by the festival orchestra: a body of artists who combine with complete mastery of all technical difficulties that intuition which alone enables the conductor to support the singers and the dramatic action, and to give full expression to the feelings aroused by complete impregnation with the demands of the drama.

The *prominence of the solo element* is a peculiarity of the *Tannhäuser* score which, partly still imbued with Weber's spirit, so frequently poses to individual players the most difficult of problems concerning sensitive delivery and delicate phrasing. Only a conductor steeped in the poetic content of the drama like Felix Mottl could, assisted by the members of the orchestra, almost conjure up before the eye of the listener in his rendering of the clarinet melody in the overture or the oboe solo passages in the preludes to Act II and III the *very characters* whose fate, as portrayed on the stage, was to compel the sympathy of the listener and to move and elate him profoundly. Only an artist with Mottl's intensity of feeling could have had the audacity to take the tempo of the 6/4 bar in the prelude to Act III as slowly as he did; because he sensed that his own fervour would inspire even the brass with the strength to play the 'Pope Scene' even at this length: *fff sustained*, as prescribed by the master.

In summing up my recollections of last year's *Tannhäuser* performance in Bayreuth, I find that the most characteristic feature of the ineffaceable impression it made on me is the *absolute perfection of style* in the playing of the *Tannhäuser* score. This rare *agreement between dramatic and musical tendency* which was capable of achievement only through the *strictest exactitude in the execution of the master's will*, precluded from the start *arbitrary behaviour* from any side, and imparted to the whole performance, by dint of the limits it set to such arbitrariness (which invariably goes hand in hand with misinterpretation), the *noble dignity* and *moving simplicity* which should be the highest aim of all truly artistic endeavour.

It is very difficult to define in words impressions made by a work of art. Nor was it my intention to do so when I felt moved to write down these short reminiscences. But very few people were privileged last year as I was to attend the festival rehearsals, thus being able to listen to the performances themselves well-

prepared for and receptive to all the subleties and beautiful passages which demand, for their full appreciation, that our eyes
and ears, spoiled as they are by a hundred years of indifferent
performances, must first be carefully attuned. It often grieved
me to see that many who were unable to attend more than one
performance, without having seen the preceding rehearsal, were
almost dazed at the idea of missing so much of what they were
accustomed to (no matter how inept that had been), whilst they
were not yet ready on the other hand to appreciate fully the
wonderful phenomenon which was being enacted before their
eyes in all its purity of style: the rebirth of the genuine *Tannhäuser*. The opera *Tannhäuser* had been *resurrected as a drama*
and, blinded by its glory, the 'Laws' of the opera, the common
tempi and the traditional canonic age of Elisabeth and many other
spectres slunk back into the obscurity of their respective Hof-
and Stadt-Theatres.

Perhaps this little pamphlet will at least succeed in drawing
the attention of men 'of good will' who will make their pilgrim-
age to Bayreuth this summer to those things which matter most
in a performance of *Tannhäuser*: Not to individual virtuoso
achievements (which are usually lacking in genuine virtuosity),
not to 'great voices', etc., but to *purity and perfection of style* as
indicated above. Nor shall I ever desist from the hope that men
will eventually discover *why we go to Bayreuth and why festivals
are organised there*. We must just have a little patience, because
in Germany everything takes a little longer than elsewhere.

Yours sincerely,

RICHARD STRAUSS.

Weimar, 1892.

ON THE 'PARSIFAL' COPYRIGHT CONTROVERSY
REPLY TO A QUESTIONNAIRE

Garmisch, August 18th, 1912.

DEAR HERR KARPATH:

The one guiding principle in the *Parsifal* controversy is, as far as I am concerned, respect for the wishes of the master.

Unfortunately, the persons called upon to settle disputes arising from the *Parsifal* copyright are not men who have the extension and intensification of our cultural life at heart, but lawyers and politicians whose vision is too limited to appreciate the unrestricted rights of the author.

I myself attended for eight days the sessions of the German Reichstag during which the representatives of the German nation, with only a very few exceptions, debated problems of copyright in enviable ignorance of the subject under discussion. I personally heard a man by the name of Eugen Richter trample under foot with the most brazen of lies the rights of two hundred German composers, including the heirs of Richard Wagner, in favour of two hundred thousand innkeepers.

These things will not change as long as we have this stupid common suffrage and as long as votes are counted and not weighed, as long as, for example, the vote of a Richard Wagner does not count for 100,000 and those of approximately 10,000 stable boys for one.

If that happened perhaps I would no longer have to hear the phrases bandied about even in the Goethe-Bund, of the rights of the German nation which is to be authorised to plunder thirty years after his death the genius whom they exiled and reviled during his lifetime and to prostitute his work on the smallest of provincial stages.

We few will protest in vain, and in two years' time the German petit bourgeois will, instead of frequenting the cinema and music-halls be able, between lunch and dinner on a Sunday afternoon, to hear *Parsifal* for sixpence.

And then we are surprised if the French and the Italians still consider us barbarians in all matters of culture.

DR. RICHARD STRAUSS.

REMARKS ON RICHARD WAGNER'S WORK AND
ON THE BAYREUTH FESTIVAL THEATRE

WHEN Richard Wagner began his gigantic work of refor-
mation with the revival and perfection of the teutonic
and Christian myths and explained his aims in spirited pamphlets, opera was in such a state that the music written by our
classics by far excelled the level of the libretti which, but for a
few exceptions such as Gluck's *Orfeo* and the two *Iphigenie*,
Fidelio, *Figaro* and *Freischütz*, never equalled the music and in
most cases fell far below it. It was only natural that he should pay
attention, assisted by his great poetic gifts, to the form of the
drama and to the scope of dramatic expression. But his attractive
idea that the chorus of the ancient drama, which accompanied
the action as critic, interpreter and guide, had been replaced by
the orchestra as created by our classical symphonic composers is
only partly correct. A superficial examination will show that the
expressive range of the modern orchestra, more especially since
Weber and Berlioz, is far greater than that of the descriptive ex-
planatory chorus of a tragedy by Aeschylus or Sophocles.

Not only does the modern orchestra paint in the background,
not only does it serve to explain and remind, but it provides the
content itself, reveals the ideal and embodies an inmost truth.
It seems intelligible that, in view of the advanced stage of development music had reached by the time of Beethoven, the talented
musician should almost take for granted the role of the orchestra
in opera but that he should have felt that everything on the stage
had to be recreated if the complete work of art which he envisaged (and which was already foreshadowed in the writings of
Goethe and Schiller) was to equal the masterpieces of these heroes
of the past or even to excel them, with the assistance of music,
so that the master was more concerned with the drama itself and

with its realisation than with the orchestra, of whose miraculous powers its creator was considerably less aware than we are.

Hence the idea of a covered invisible orchestra which I consider to be justified and beautifully effective only in *Parsifal* and, after my own experiences at Bayreuth especially in the years 1889 to 1894, in *Tristan* and *Der Ring*. Admittedly voice and word are used to better effect in the festival theatre than in a theatre with a visible, and, frequently, a raised orchestra. But many of the inexhaustible riches of the score are lost at Bayreuth —I need only remind you of *Die Meistersinger*. And in which, after all, is a civilised audience more interested: in the opera and the singers? Or in the orchestra? I think the latter. Nor do I believe that I am only speaking of myself as a listener and spectator. When I have seen *Wallenstein* or *Iphigenie* three times I know the poem, and after three performances I also know *Tristan*; and from then on the only things which interest me on the stage are a conscientious new production or new singers.

The orchestra in *Tristan* and in *Die Meistersinger*, on the other hand, no matter how carefully and frequently I study the score at home, reveals something new every time: I suppose I have heard *Parsifal* and *Der Ring* fifty times each (usually when I myself have been rehearsing and conducting) yet I cannot have enough of the revelations of this orchestra and I discover in it new beauties and am grateful for new revelations every time. The producers and stage designers who consider that a brightly lit orchestra pit and brilliantly illuminated conductor's rostrum detract from cleverly-lit stage-settings are therefore against me. It does not disturb me to see in front of me an orchestra playing well and a conductor who really leads and inspires it (his movements must not, however, be too fidgety), if this little sacrifice means that not a single wonderful detail in the magic carpet of *Die Meistersinger* score is lost and that I am in a position to enjoy an ideal concord between stage and orchestra, such as it has been my privilege to experience not only in Vienna and Salzburg (and under Clemens Krauss in Munich), but also in Berlin and Dresden under Leo Blech and Karl Böhm. I know many music enthusiasts who share this opinion. In short, let us make our pilgrimage to Bayreuth in order to hear *Tristan* and *Parsifal*, to do homage to the great master and to hear these operas as he expressly desired them to be heard and seen. On the whole I am more in favour of the old Italian theatre. But with this reservation: the orchestra must consist of eighty to one hundred players; 16 first and 16 second violins, 12 violas, 12 'celli, and 8 double basses.

[*ca.* 1940]

ON MOZART'S *COSÍ FAN TUTTE*

*W**RITTEN on the occasion of the new production from the original in Munich.*

The great Mozart's last opera buffa *Cosí fan tutte* has had a curious fate and, of all the dramatic works of the master, it has so far been the most neglected by producers as well as audiences. On the whole it would, I suppose, be true to say that the average opinion of *Cosí fan tutte,* is that this opera, although it contains a number of extremely beautiful pieces such as the famous Addio quintet, the finale of the first act and two very popular arias of Despina, is, taken as a whole, a comparatively weak work of Mozart. Even Richard Wagner considered that Mozart's usually so elastic wings had been clipped, especially in the second act, by this bad libretto. Although I agree with Richard Wagner that the fable as such is not particularly intelligent, I would point out that, quite apart from the almost impossible hypothesis demanded by the action, the psychological development of the plot is not by any means without interest, particularly if one considers the time at which the libretto was written. Works by great masters, handicapped by weaknesses in the dramatic structure or in the libretto, have always fallen an easy prey to 'intelligent' directors and producers. The harmless ones amongst them are content to refrain from performing those works which are bound to be financial failures, whereas the more dangerous are in the habit of editing them: a process referred to in the language of the stage as 'making' a play. In the case of *Cosí fan tutte* in particular, conductors have usually, following the old traditions of the stage, found a way out by cutting all the numbers and any *recitativo secco* which did not seem to represent Mozart at his best to those music enthusiasts who, departing from the usual custom, applied the standards of the stage to Mozart's operas. It was especially

amongst the *recitativo secco* passages which, since they belonged
purely to the action of the play, did not provide the musical feast
the above-mentioned music enthusiasts expected, although in
Così fan tutte more than elsewhere Mozart treated them with the
greatest possible diligence and provided them with the most
charming of touches, that the blue pencil was allowed to run
amok.

To have given Mozart an opportunity of evolving this particular style is the great merit of Lorenzo da Ponte, the author of
Così fan tutte, which notwithstanding a few improbabilities,
occupies a fairly high position amongst the libretti of the time,
as already pointed out by Otto Jahn, and which excels by a long
way, especially as far as the careful evolution of a purely psychological plot is concerned, most of the other libretti of Mozart's
operas with the sole exception of *Figaro*. In this particular use of
the language of sound contrasting the exaggerated, almost comic,
but quite genuine pathos of the two ladies on the one hand with
the hollow phrases of the two lovers in disguise on the other who,
whilst singing inspired love-duets with their vanquished fiancées,
are consumed in their very vitals by seething anger at the incon-
stancy of these same fiancées, Mozart's art of characterization
reached its zenith. Not only is *Così fan tutte* unique amongst
Mozart's dramatic masterpieces, it is also one of the gems of the
whole of operatic comedy prior to Richard Wagner's *Meistersinger*. Why, then has it not won the same public acclaim as
Figaro, *Don Giovanni* and *The Magic Flute*? It may be that at a
time when, to satisfy the purely musical tastes of the audience,
singers concentrated their attention on doing justice to the musical style of an opera, the peculiar parodic style of Mozart's
comedy did not achieve the dramatic effect intended by its
author and composer. The very pieces which expressed this style
most clearly, namely the E flat major aria of Dorabella in the
first Act, Fernando's B flat major aria and Guglielmo's aria in G

major in the second Act with their connecting and extremely charming recitativos, were invariably cut because they were obviously considered as musically inferior, although in reality they are all the most interesting and important from the dramatic point of view.

Garmisch, 16th December [1910]

ON MOZART

IT has become customary to treat this, the most sublime of all composers, as a 'rococo artist' and to present his works as the essence of grace and playfulness. Although it is true that he is the composer who solved all 'problems' as it were, before they were even raised, and that he divested passion of all earthly taint, attaining so to speak, a bird's eye view of it, his work, although it is transfigured, ethereal and far from harsh reality, embraces the entire range of human emotions, from the monumental and gloomy grandeur of the supper scene in *Don Giovanni* to the delicacy of the arias of Zerlina, the heavenly frivolity of *Figaro* and the detached irony of *Così fan tutte*. If not to the same extent, but with no less intensity, his non-dramatic creations run the whole gamut of human emotion. It is senseless as well as superficial to postulate a uniform Mozartian style for the performance of these infinitely delicate and highly articulate psychological studies.

*   *   *

In Susanna's garden aria, in Belmonte's and Ferrando's A major arias, in Octavio's G major, Eros himself speaks to us in Mozart's melody, love addresses itself to our emotions in its most beautiful and purest form. Zerlina's two arias are not the utterances of a common farmer's daughter fallen a prey to seduction. In the slow passage of Donna Anna's so-called 'Letter' aria and in the two arias of the Countess in *Figaro*, we have ideal creations which I can only compare with Plato's 'Ideas', the ideal prototype of the forms projected into the natural world.

*   *   *

Mozart follows as a miracle almost immediately after Bach with the perfection and absolute idealisation of the melody of the human voice—I would call them Platonic 'Ideas' and 'Prototypes', not to be seen by the eye nor grasped by reason, but so essentially divine that they are to be intuitively perceived only by the emotions, which the ear enables to 'breathe them in'. Untrammelled by any mundane form, the Mozartian melody is the 'Ding an sich'. It hovers like Plato's Eros between heaven and earth, between mortality and immortality—set free from 'the Will'—it is the deepest penetration of artistic fancy and of the subconscious into the uttermost secrets, into the realm of the 'prototypes'.

[1944]

ON JOHANN STRAUSS

OF all god-gifted dispensers of joy, Johann Strauss is to me the most endearing. That first, comprehensive statement can serve as a text for everything I feel about this wonderful phenomenon. In particular I respect in Johann Strauss his originality, his innate gift. At a time when the whole world around him was tending towards increased complexity, increased reflectiveness, his natural genius enabled him to create from the *whole*. He seemed to me the last of those who worked from spontaneous inspiration. Yes, the primary, the original, the protomelody, that's it. . . .

Also, I saw him and talked with him and visited him in Munich at the 'Vier Jahrenzeiten'. But I really got to know and to love the whole realm of his wisdom in Meiningen, through Hans von Bülow, who had a beautifully bound collection of all the Strauss waltzes. Once he played them to me for an entire evening. For me alone, and unforgettable evening of waltzes! I also willingly admit to having sometimes conducted the *Perpetuum mobile* with far more pleasure than many a four movement symphony. And as for the *Rosenkavalier* waltzes . . . how could I have done those without a thought of the laughing genius of Vienna?

[1925]

GUSTAV MAHLER

IN my opinion, Gustav Mahler's work is one of the most important and most interesting products of our modern history of art.
Just as I was one of the first to have the privilege of championing
his symphonic creations before the public, I consider it to be one
of my most pleasant duties to obtain for them in future both in
word and deed that general recognition which is their pre-
eminent desert. The plastic of his orchestration in particular, is
absolutely exemplary.

[1910]

COMMEMORATIVE ADDRESS ON FRIEDRICH RÖSCH

IT is particularly difficult to address you after hearing the moving strains of an immortal masterpiece*. Rarely has anyone been more worthy of being apostrophised. The remarkable man, all too soon torn from our midst, whom we are today laying to his rest with deepest sorrow, was a companion of my youth and has been my most faithful friend and mentor for a whole generation. I have always owed recreation, inspiration and stimulation to his unshakable loyalty, his all-embracing knowledge, his insuperable idealism and his truly productive and acute criticism. Irreplaceable as he was, he left me without saying farewell and it is only at his grave that I can return thanks to him for everything he gave me.

By dint of his great gifts, his talent for organisation, the depth of his knowledge, his strength of character and his originality, Friedrich Rösch was destined to fulfil a lofty calling in the service of his German fatherland, and if Richard Wagner's saying, 'To be German means to do a thing for its own sake', may be allowed to stand, he was a genuine and great German. He preferred to put all his gifts at the service of the German composers. What he has achieved in this respect will not only be engraved in our grateful hearts to all eternity, it is recorded in the annals of the history of German music. It is impossible to do full justice here to his life's task. I would, however, like to draw your attention briefly to two all-important aspects of his life's work: Friedrich Rösch wrestled with the legislators for the rights of the German composer and it is to him that the latter owes his dignity and independence of the publisher. Rösch, who was a fanatic of selflessness and, I may say, a saint in his self-sacrifice,

---

*Beethoven's Egmont Overture.

dedicated all his energies, his fortune, his health and his life to his work. We can only repay him by vowing here and now to continue his work as he would wish us to continue it, never letting out of our sight the final goal which he has set us, never deviating by so much as an inch from the path which he has mapped out.

In view of this solemn promise, which I make in the presence of his faithful wife, the earth I know, will rest lightly upon him.

Farewell, dear friend, and rest in peace!

[1925]

ON THE MUNICH OPERA

THE most pleasant memories of my youth are connected with Munich opera and its wonderful orchestra, of which my father was, for more than forty years, an adornment whom even Richard Wagner praised and who, under Hermann Levi, played to Richard Strauss in his 'teens his D minor symphony.

All the great impressions made by the classical masterpieces, from the first performance I heard of *Der Freischütz*—how terrified I was, at the age of eight, by the appearance of Zamiel—to *Tristan* which, at the age of fifteen, I did not understand at all, and the first performance of *Siegfried* that I attended, squashed like a sardine in the gods, amidst groans of discomfort, are engraved in my memory owing to the high artistic level of the performances of the Munich Court Theatre.

When I was called to Munich as 'Musikdirektor' from Meiningen in the year 1887, and won my spurs with *Johann von Paris*, and *Così fan tutte* (I can still see Heinrich Vogl standing in front of me saying, 'Strauss, your movements are too sweeping, and your conducting arm is too long'), joys alternated with sorrows in the career of the comparatively unpractised outsider I then was. A blunder I made in *Czar und Zimmermann* and which disturbed me frequently, even in my dreams, the production of Richard Wagner's *Feen*, the direction of which was taken out of my hands just before the dress rehearsal by Herr von Perfall, to be entrusted to Herr Fischer, with the remark that a first performance of such importance could not be conducted by 'the third conductor', the anxieties I suffered during the first performance of my opera *Guntram*, which had to be taken off the repertoire after the first performance because the tenor declared he could only go on singing his very taxing part if he were provided contractually with a higher pension: these and several other contretemps belong to the second and less pleasing category of my experience in Munich.

But *Tristan* and *Die Meistersinger* which I was allowed to conduct for the first time in the consecrated place of their birth as early as 1894, when I was recalled as Court Conductor from Weimar, and the Mozart Festival I inaugurated with Possart (only *Figaro* had still been rehearsed by Levi) still remain as shining memories in my life.

[1928]

CONGRATULATORY ADDRESS TO THE
VIENNA PHILHARMONIC

Vienna, 18th February, 1942.

Dear members of the Philharmonic, I can only congratulate you with heartfelt words on your Jubilee today. The musical offering I had intended to give you, my dear friends and fellow-artists, on this rare occasion, has not, I am afraid, been completed, no matter how hard I have tried. Emotions are not as readily transmuted into melodies as in the days of the grand old masters. I would, therefore, ask you to have patience until my gift shall become worthy of its recipient so that it may remain in your memories as a living expression of my love and my admiration. To praise the Philharmonic Orchestra would be to carry violins to Vienna, but I value the *piano* of the woodwinds, the splendour of the harps and the inexorable kettle drum no less.

Your artistic achievements are acclaimed by enthusiastic audiences the world over. I wish to formulate my praise today in one short sentence: 'Only he who has *conducted* the Vienna Philharmonic knows what it is.'

But let that be a secret between you and me.

I know you will understand me, here as well as at the conductor's rostrum!

With a thousand good wishes, your grateful and faithful

DR. RICHARD STRAUSS.

CONGRATULATORY ADDRESS TO THE STATE ORCHESTRA OF SAXONY

Pontresina, 25th July, 1948.

To the honourable members of the State Orchestra of Saxony.

Far from home, in Richard Wagner's refuge, I received the news that the Dresden State Orchestra, which has amongst others been consecrated by the great master, is celebrating the four hundredth anniversary of its foundation, a Jubilee which may well be unique in the history of music. I consider it to be my rare good fortune to be allowed to communicate to such a wonderful community of artists my heartiest and most sincere congratulations on this auspicious occasion.

It must be more than fifty years ago that thirteen eminent woodwind players of this orchestra launched my little serenade in the Dresden Tonkünstlerverein, and fifty years since I heard a perfect performance of my *Don Juan* in Sempers magnificent opera house, under Hagen's baton. Then, under the indefatigable wand of the inspired Schuch, began the series of exemplary first performances: *Feuersnot, Salome, Elektra,* and *Rosenkavalier,* to which my operatic work owes its greatest successes, due largely to the selfless achievements of this orchestra. From the store of the most cherished memories of my artistic career, the performances of this masterly orchestra never fail to evoke anew the feelings of heartfelt gratitude and admiration with which I invariably and, for the last time in June 1944, left the beloved theatre. May good fortune, blessings and new laurels in keeping with its four-hundred-year-old tradition be the lot of the State Orchestra in its new home, where my opera *Intermezzo* was first performed.

Yours as ever,

DR. RICHARD STRAUSS.

CONTEMPORARY REMARKS ON MUSICAL EDUCATION
For a Teacher Friend

SOME two thousand five hundred years ago the great Confucius formulated the principles of Chinese ethics in three fundamental tenets:

(*a*) Cult of one's ancestors, i.e. pious conservation and study of the achievements of our forefathers.

(*b*) Cultivation of good manners, i.e. our relationship with our fellow men.

(*c*) Cultivation of music, i.e. achievement of an inner harmony.

We cannot tell to-day how the Chinese music sounded which this philosopher himself so assiduously practised and the cultivation of which he considered to be so important in the training and education of civilized man, but we see how the art of music from Johann Sebastian Bach to Richard Wagner has captivated the heart of the whole civilized world and is even capable to-day, through the somewhat problematic medium of wireless, if not to delight our ears, at least to help to overcome the boredom of empty evenings.

But in what does this so-called enjoyment of art consist, as far as the majority of listeners to music are concerned? Is it a purely sensual aural feast, unmitigated by any mental activity? One listener may be excited by the beauty of sound of a high tenor voice, another by the brio of a Beethoven stretta, a third admires the laryngeal attainments of a coloratura soprano, or the power and speed of the concert pianist; at the sound of a Stradivarius violin he is filled with a sense of well-being; he is pleased with himself if he can glean a more or less intelligible melody from the otherwise intolerable pandemonium of a classical symphony; he heaves a sigh of relief if after four dissonant hours of *Tristan* —after 'all that fuss about the steamer' as a good lady of Hamburg was once heard to complain at the great climax of the Liebestod with its unequalled magic of sound (the last bar is considered to be the most beautifully scored last chord in the history of music) he leaves the theatre in moderately high animal spirits. But when I ask dozens of these concert enthusiasts, enamoured with the wonderful movements and the rapturous bearing of their favourite conductor, what it is that they have heard they will in nine cases out of ten reply 'Well, . . . the Ninth Symphony, it was wonderful, but the soloists weren't much good'; or 'the Jupiter Symphony with the "famous" fugue'; '*The Trout* Quintet'; 'the Unfinished Symphony'; 'the *Drum-Roll* symphony'. Or, after a performance of *Die Meistersinger*: What did you like best? may receive the answer '*Am stillen Herd*', 'the *Preislied*', or at best, 'the quintet and the pompous overture'; —after *Die Walküre*: 'Winterstürme wichen dem Wonnemond', and 'especially the "Feuerzauber".' What it really is that the great public has heard, of what the great impression made by the Eroica symphony or by the C sharp minor Quartet consisted; what it is in one of Mozart's *Figaro*—or *Così fan tutte*—finales that is deserving of enthusiasm, listeners will not be able to say, unless they are to some extent proficient pianists or, as some of them do to this day in Vienna, play chamber music as practising amateurs on a Sunday afternoon, thus bringing a receptive mind trained by long practice to abstract music. What constitutes the highest worth of the masterly creations of music (the last art to be brought to perfection) can only be determined by those who have been apprenticed to the discipline of harmony and counterpoint, and who when reading a score by Wagner or Berlioz can hear it with the ears of the spirit so that all the various nuances in the treatment of the woodwind in *Lohengrin* or *Die Walküre*, the profound secrets of the orchestra in Wotam's recitative, really become a source of the highest artistic enjoyment.

Music is a language which the layman thinks he can understand better than, for example, Turkish, since its few letters are more easily learned by heart than are those of the Koran and since the natural ear finds it easier to remember a simple melody of eight bars and considers it more euphonious than a sentence of Chinese. From this second year onward, any child learns his mother-tongue by play and imitation. When he leaves the elementary school he can read what books he chooses. If only by constant comparison the human eye is trained so quickly that a twelve-year-old school boy can distinguish a Madonna from a Saint Sebastian in the picture-gallery, whilst assiduous reading of titles saves him from the embarrassment of mistaking a Ruisdael for a Corot, or a Titian for a Rembrandt. But does that mean that he has any real idea of how a real work of art is distinguished from the most common and garish of trash? Is he in a position to determine why one of Menzel's Sanssouci scenes is a better painting than Anton von Werner's *Kaiserkrönung in Versailles*? If on entering St. Stephen's Cathedral he feels the same powerful religious emotion as when he listens to the Kyrie in Bach's B minor mass, and if when listening to a Beethoven adagio he lapses into a dreamy mood in which, at best, his fancy allows him to see vague visions, will he immediately be in a position to recognise the full artistic import of a Gothic cathedral or of the *Meistersinger* score and will he be able to enjoy them as such? Since he is at least familiar with language, the *Wallenstein* trilogy or, if he has eyes in his head, the Sistine Madonna will give him more aesthetic enjoyment than one of the later Beethoven Quartets, whose austerity of sound will be unlikely to evoke in him the same sense of well-being as that provided by listening to the *Lohengrin* prelude, magnificently scored and endowed as it is with a grand and instinctively exciting climax. Any layman, after hearing a poem by Schiller, at least knows what he has been listening to. But this is simply not the case with a Mozart Quartet.

Our humanist curriculum is still based on subjects whose study, prior to the invention of modern music, was a necessary precondition for a higher education. To this day it is weighed down with unnecessary study of higher mathematics, elementary chemistry and physics, which could safely be left to those students in our universities and technical colleges who wish to make a profession of them. The study of music, which has so far been completely neglected at all our secondary schools, is an essential element of all higher education, at least to the extent of learning sufficient harmony and counterpoint for the appreciation of a Bach fugue and sufficient orchestration to understand fully the psychological and contrapuntal struggles in the third act of *Tristan*, or the structure and development of subjects in the movement of a Beethoven symphony, and the symphonic structure of an act from the *Ring des Nibelungen*.

If these studies were carried out systematically by at least those scholars in secondary schools who are not completely unmusical, and who, if possible, play an instrument—the others could be referred for semi-professional studies to the plastic arts—they would discover treasures of artistic enjoyment. It would be a work of great merit to carry out a reform of our secondary schools in this direction.

[1933]

LETTER ON THE *HUMANISTISCHE GYMNASIUM*

To PROFESSOR REISINGER,

IT was with great interest that I read your valuable lecture on the teaching of the history of languages (*Süddeutsche Monatshefte*, 1910) and I should therefore be glad if you would allow me to declare myself in full agreement with it. At a time when 'the teaching of mathematics and the sciences' has in the course of two world wars been reduced *ad absurdum*—let us hope for good—in the destructive fury of the much celebrated 'technology', the call of Culture for humanistic education is to be welcomed and supported more than ever.

As far as I myself am concerned, I cannot say that I was a particularly good pupil of the Ludwigsgymnasium in Munich, especially since, musically precocious, I was always fonder of composing than of studying, but nevertheless I managed to pass my matriculation examination without discredit at the age of eighteen; it was only in mathematics that I failed, because I could not come to terms with algebra. But a love of Greece and of the ancient world has remained with me and has increased ever since 1892, when, thanks to the generosity of my good uncle the brewer Georg Pschorr, I was able to go to Egypt for eight months to restore my health, which had been threatened by two attacks of pneumonia. On the way to Egypt I spent three weeks in Greece. From the moment when, coming from Brindisi, I saw from the deck of the Italian steamer the island of Corfu and the blue mountains of Albania, I have always been a German Greek, even to this day.

For I can look back on artistic achievements which, like *Elektra*, *Ariadne*, *Aegyptische Helena*, *Daphne*, and *Die Liebe der Danae*, do homage to the genius of the Greek nation, and it is with pride that I sign myself with the title 'Honorary Freeman of the Isle of Naxos' bestowed on me some twenty years ago, and with pleasure that I remember the award of the Grand Cross of the Greek order of Christ.

The wisdom of China and of India has survived for thousands of years and the artistic urge of the orient has erected in the majestic buildings of Babylon and Egypt eternal monuments to profound religions. Within sight of the blue Aegean and under the famous 'eternally blue and radiant sky', Greek sculpture bestowed a marble immortality upon the human form, while the Greek poets gave immortal form in Epic and Drama to *mythus*—born of inspired imagination, sprung like Pallas Athene from the head of Zeus—and the Greek philosophers, driven by profound curiosity, blazed a path for science, for thousands of years to come. Greece was that happy soil where for the first time a civilisation was able to grow which, fostered by the moderating influence of the Central European climate and by the wealth and beauty of the landscape, has by its inspiration given to humanity eternal spiritual achievements from Dante, Michelangelo, Raphael, Grünewald, Shakespeare, Kant, Schopenhauer, Schiller, and many others, to the greatest of them all, Goethe.

After the creation of German music by Johann Sebastian Bach, after the revelation of the human soul (sought for by all philosophers since Plato) in Mozart's melody—which I would like to compare with Plato's Eros hovering between heaven and earth— and after the magnificent palaces of Beethoven's symphonies, Richard Wagner, the poet-dramatist and philosopher-musician, at last completed a cultural development of three thousand years by creating the language of the modern orchestra, thus fulfilling the German Christian myth in perfect music-dramatic creations.

In order not only to perceive intuitively the great works of art of the master of Bayreuth and the creations of the geniuses of music who went before him, but to appreciate them in their full importance, we require a musical education which has in the past been available only to the exceptionally gifted in the conservatoires of music. The remainder of humanity sits in our opera houses and concert-halls in the shape of the so-called 'artistic public', very much like a ten-year-old at a performance of *Wallenstein* in Chinese. The fact that music, too, has become a language capable of every poetic expression—especially by means of the sound symbols of the mysterious body of instruments (called the orchestra) once endowed by Josef Haydn with the human soul— is, in its last perfection, the divine achievement of Wagner's scores. To be able to penetrate into this 'realm of the mothers' requires above all a long musical education without which even the greatest endeavours of the 'Gymnasium' remain inadequate. The last chapter 'German music since Johann Sebastian Bach' must not be missing from its library.

The major achievements of humanism had been reached before the birth of 'modern music'. It is left to a future generation —and may a creative musician be allowed to recommend this task to the educators of a younger generation which is called upon to rebuild a culture now almost completely destroyed—to incorporate this serious musical education in the syllabus of the *Humanistische Gymnasium*. If the senior scholar is capable, just as he can read Homer and Horace in the original, and understand the *Wahlverwandtschaften* or *Faust* or, if he is an Englishman, *Hamlet*, of appreciating fully a Beethoven symphony, a Mozart quintet or the prelude to *Die Meistersinger* or *Tristan*, if he can survey the structure of these edifices of sound in all their greatness and if he has moreover learned to read the language of music, he will have laid those foundations of education which will enable him to give of his best in accordance with his talents. Not until then will the *Humanistische Gymnasium* have done its duty in the formation of the mind and soul of man. I would refer you to a valuable essay written in the year 1848 in which Ferdinand

Kürnberger, the Viennese author of the important novel *Der Amerikamüde* says: 'If you cannot read a score you cannot read at all!'—I would not be so bold as to enumerate the shortcomings of the *Humanistische Gymnasium* of to-day—they have been discussed by men better qualified than I; but I must admit that I myself considered the training of memory encouraged in the teaching of history and the exaggerated importance given to grammar to be reprehensible, so that I completely agree with Professor Reisinger's suggestion that it would be better, instead of spending months in deciphering Homer's periods and their grammatical peculiarities in isolated books, to let the pupils themselves recite the whole of the *Iliad* and *Odyssey* as well as the *Oresteia* and *Oedipus* in good German translations (with explanations by the teacher); this would be preferable to allowing the schoolboy to leave school (as happened to me) with the knowledge of a very few but personally translated extracts. I further agree that elementary studies in physics and chemistry, geology, etc., if only because of the tremendous scope of these specialised sciences, are an unnecessary burden for secondary schools; but I consider the suggestion made by Professor Cornelius regarding elementary studies of jurisprudence extremely interesting. I consider some knowledge of the law to be part of the fundamental structure of a higher education, like Latin, Greek, German, Mathematics, and Music.

The oldest Chinese religion (Confucius) already contains as one of its three fundamental postulates 'the cultivation of music'. I therfore recommend that in the syllabus of the sixth forms, three hours a week (one hour of theory, two of pianoforte playing) be devoted to music. If that happened two-thirds of the students of the *Humanistische Gymnasium* would form, in five to ten years' time, the nucleus of a concert and theatre audience before whom it would really be worthwhile to perform *Tristan* and who would listen to a Schubert symphony or the fugue in the Jupiter symphony with as much attention as to *Nathan der Weise* or *Die Jungfrau von Orleans.*

Let no one say that my suggestion could only work with musically talented scholars. The abstract study of harmony and counterpoint including the 'mathematical problems' of the fugue is easier to master than algebra and the fundamental concepts of chemistry and physics, and in the long run they represent a greater source of enjoyment in the life of the pupil than an elementary knowledge of science, which is useless to him unless he specialises in science at the university. Any pupil who completely fails in the theoretical study of music before it enters the realm of immediate sound conceptions—i.e. before the study of orchestration and scoring—must of course be enabled in time to change over to the study of mathematics and science within the narrow scope given to these in the *Humanistische Gymnasium.*

May the *Humanistische Gymnasium*, in the competent hands of experienced friends and enriched by music, soon be resurrected in its pristine glory as the Benevolent guardian of European culture.

[Summer 1945]

ON *JOSEPHSLEGENDE*

M Y intention in *Josephslegende* was to revive the dance. The dance, the mother of the arts, standing, as it were, like a mediator between them. The dance as an expression of the dramatic, but not only of the dramatic. The modern variant of the dance, in which it is nothing but rhythmic or paraphrased action, only too frequently leads us away from the essence of the genuine, purely inspirational, form of the dance dedicated to movement and to absolute beauty, i.e. the ballet. It was this that I intended to rejuvenate. I think it was the Russian dancers who first put the idea into my head. My *Joseph* contains both elements: Dance as drama and dance as—dance. We must not lose the sense of the purely graceful just as, analogously, in the realm of music the element of absolute beauty must never be neglected in favour of the characteristic, programmatic and elemental. This, if you will, was my intention in writing *Josephslegende*.

[1941]

PREFACE TO *INTERMEZZO*

IN classical opera there are two methods of managing the dialogue which serves to develop the plot: pure prose or the so-called *reictativo secco* with cembalo accompaniment. Only Beethoven and Marschner effectively used an emotional melodrama in important passages. In Mozart's German operas the plot proper is almost exclusively expressed in spoken prose followed without transition by vocal music in the form of songs, ensembles in somewhat freer form, the great finales elaborated into somewhat longer symphonic compositions, and the arias preceded by an orchestral recitativo (*recitativo accompagnato*) all of which are inclined to slow down the action. Apart from Gluck's operas and Nicolai's *Merry Wives*, *The Magic Flute* alone contains a recitative passage of greater length which really serves to develop the action: the great scene between Tamino and the priest: a scene which constitutes the zenith of Mozart's dramatic work. In his Italian operas Mozart adopted the *recitativo secco* from the *opera buffa*, with the considerable improvement in *Così fan tutte*, of allowing the orchestra to play the accompaniment at times when the dialogue contains lyrical passages.

These brief remarks should suffice to remind experts with what care our great masters treated the dialogue on which the action on the whole depends. But it is striking that none of our classical composers made use of the subtle nuances which may result from the development from ordinary prose via melodrama, *recitativo secco*, and *recitativo accompagnato* to the unimpeded flow of the melody of a song.

Perhaps it was inevitable that the peculiar subject matter taken completely from real life and embracing the whole gamut from the sober prose of every-day life through the various shades of dialogue to sentimental song, should induce me, who had in my previous works taken much care to render the dialogue natural, to adopt the style realised in *Intermezzo*.

I have always paid the greatest possible attention to natural diction and speed of dialogue, with increasing success from opera to opera. While in my first opera *Guntram* the distinction, so carefully observed by Richard Wagner, between passages which are merely recited and those which are purely lyrical, was almost completely neglected, the dialogue in *Salome* and *Elektra* was largely rescued from being drowned by the symphonic orchestra. But it is unfortunately still very much handicapped by instrumental polyphony unless extremely careful observation of my dynamic markings gives the orchestra that pellucidity which I took for granted when composing the operas, and which I know from perfect performances to be capable of achievement.

But since it is indeed rare that we can count on such ideal performances on the stage, I found myself more and more compelled to secure from the start the balance between singer and orchestra to such an extent that even in less perfect performances the action above all should, at least in broad outline, be plain and easily intelligible, lest the opera be disfigured or open to misrepresentation. The scores of *Die Frau ohne Schatten* and *Ariadne* are the fruits of these endeavours.

In the former I attempted, especially in the part of the nurse, to inject new life into the style and pace of the old *recitativo secco* by means of an orchestral accompaniment using mainly solo instruments and filling in the background with light strokes. Unfortunately, this attempt did not succeed in making the dialogue, which is of the utmost importance particularly in these scenes, absolutely clear.

The fault may lie either in a lack of talent on my part, as a result of which even this tenuous and diaphanous orchestra appears still too polyphonous, and its figuring so erratic as to impede the spoken word on the stage, or it may be due to the imperfect diction on the part of the majority of our operatic singers, or again to the unfortunately often guttural tone of German singers, or to the excessive forcing of sound on our big stages.

There can be no doubt that orchestral polyphony, no matter how subdued its tones or how softly it is played, spells death to the spoken word on the stage, and the devil himself is to blame that we Germans imbibe counterpoint with our mothers' milk, to keep us from being too successful on the operatic stage.

Not even our greatest dramatic master succeeded in creating 'ideal recitativos' except in *Lohengrin* and *Rheingold*, so that no listener will ever be able to enjoy the poetry of the text, no matter how subdued the orchestral playing, in the great polyphonous symphonies of the second act of *Tristan* and the third act of *Siegfried*.

Anybody who knows my later operatic scores well, will have to admit that, provided the singer pronounces the words clearly and the dynamic markings in the score are strictly observed, the words of the text must be clearly understood by the listener, except in a few passages where these words may permissibly be drowned by the orchestra as it plays with increasing intensity for the purpose of pointing a necessary climax. No praise pleases me more than when after I have conducted *Elektra* somebody says to me: 'To-night I understood every word': if this is not the case you may safely assume that the orchestral score was not played in the manner exactly prescribed by me.

On this occasion I should like to draw attention to the peculiar nature of the dynamic markings I use in my scores. I am no longer content with prescribing *pp*, *p*, *f*, *ff*, for the whole orchestra, but give a large variety of dynamic markings for individual groups and even individual instruments, the exact observance of which, although it is the main requirement for the correct performance of my orchestral scores, presupposes indeed the existence of a type of orchestral discipline which is somewhat rare to-day, but is absolutely necessary for a performance of my scores in accordance with my intentions. Special attention should be paid to the accurate execution of *fp* and of every *expressivo* calling for a frequently all but unnoticeable preponderance of one part over its neighbours. Only thus can finely articulated polyphony be clearly represented. If one particular part predominates, important subsidiary strands may be destroyed.

The more polyphonous and complicated a score, the more necessary would it seem to be for each player to observe the dynamic markings of his part irrespective of those in the score of his neighbour in the orchestra. To illustrate my point I would like to quote here some remarks made by Hans von Bülow: '*Crescendo* means *pp*, *diminuendo* means *ff*', and 'Most conductors are incapable of reading scores'. He wrote in the album of a famous tenor 'a crotchet is no quaver'. During an orchestral rehearsal in Meiningen he shouted at the first horn player '*forte*': the latter blew harder. Bülow interrupted and said with gentle rebuke, 'I said *forte*': the horn player blew harder still. Bülow, interrupting for the third time and raising his voice: 'First horn, *forte*', to which the horn player replied in despair, 'But, sir, I can't blow any harder'. Bülow then said with a mephistophelian smile and utmost suavity of voice: 'That is exactly what I mean, I keep asking you to play *forte* and you go on playing *fortissimo*'. General hubbub. From that day onward the difference between *f* and *ff* had been finally established. Many sad experiences increased my desire to prevent at all costs one of these virtuosos of the rostrum from rousing the brass to a frenzy with his fists, and from degrading the singers to mere grimacers, relying on the indestructibility of a *Tristan* or *Meistersinger* score.

No rendering of the orchestral part, however brilliant and noisy, given by one of the many concert-hall conductors who have unfortunately nowadays taken to conducting opera can silence the just complaints against such aural feasts at the expense of the intelligibility of plot and libretto.

It was out of this necessity that the score of *Ariadne* was born. The orchestra has not been relegated to the rôle of accompanist and yet, in spite of the expressive force of the 'chamber orchestra', the sounds and words uttered by the singer are bound to be intelligible in any performance, no matter how heartless the officiating conductor may be.

It was in the first act of *Ariadne* that I first used with full assurance, in the alternation between ordinary prose, *recitativo secco* and *recitativo accompagnato*, the vocal style which I have now, in *Intermezzo*, carried to its logical conclusion. But in none of my other works is the dialogue of greater importance than in this bourgeois comedy, which offers few chances to the deployment of the so-called *cantilena*. The symphonic element has been so carefully and repeatedly revised and polished that in many instances it is merely hinted at and cannot, even when dynamic markings are carelessly observed, prevent the natural conversational tone, derived and copied from everyday life, from being not only heard but also clearly understood, this applies to the context as well as to each individual word; the lyrical element, the description of the spiritual experiences of the *dramatis personae* is developed mainly in the comparatively long orchestral interludes. Not until the final scenes of the first and second acts is the singer really given a chance of extended *cantilena*.

Wherever the dialogue contains lyrical elements in the other scenes, the singers as well as the conductor should carefully distinguish between *cantilena* and *recitativo*, and the listener must be able to follow the natural flow of the conversation without interruption and must be able to follow clearly all the subtle variations in the development of the characters as portrayed in the opera; if he fails to do so, the performance will have the effect of intolerable tedium since the listener, inadequately under-

standing the text, will not be able to comprehend the plot in all
its details, nor will the musically trained ear find sufficient com-
pensation in symphonic orgies.

The singer in particular should remember that only a properly
formed consonant will penetrate even the most brutal of orchestras, whereas the strongest note of the human voice, even when
singing the best vowel 'ah', will be drowned without difficulty by
an orchestra of eighty or a hundred players playing no louder than
mezzo forte. The singer has only one weapon against a polyphonous and indiscreet orchestra: the consonant. I have myself
seen it happen, especially in Wagner's music dramas, e.g. in
Wotan's Narration and in the Erda scene of *Siegfried*, that singers
with great voices but poor diction were left to flounder impotently
in the waves of orchestral sound, whereas singers with considerably weaker voices but decisive pronunciation of consonants,
could carry the poet's words victoriously and without the slightest
difficulty against the maelstrom of the symphonic orchestra.

I would, on the other hand, ask the conductor when rehearsing
Intermezzo to pay the greatest attention to the gradual transition
from the spoken word to the sung and half-spoken word, to all
the subtle turns in the conversation where prose hesitates between
recitativo secco and the style of *recitativo accompagnato*, to reach
its climax at last in the so-called *bel canto* in which absolute clarity
could at times be sacrificed to beauty of intonation. The chief
precept for the practical execution of the *Intermezzo* dialogue is
that all passages of pure dialogue—in so far as they do not change
for short periods of time into lyrical outpourings of emotions—in
other words, all passages resembling *recitativo secco*, should be
presented *mezza voce* throughout. Practical experience teaches us
that with full volume the precision of pronunciation and especially the formation of consonants suffer considerably. This is
illustrated by the fact—known to every expert on the theatre—
that during orchestral rehearsals even in an empty theatre, which

is acoustically unfavourable, every word of the singers singing *mezza voce* can usually be understood, whereas barely half the words are understood when they sing with full voice during the performance. Therefore, my dear singers, if you wish to be good actors as well, sing *mezza voce* and pronounce your words clearly, and the orchestra will automatically accompany you better and the public will enjoy listening to you in this harmless comedy more than if, struggling in vain against a superior enemy, you strain your vocal chords unnecessarily for the sake of an opera from which you cannot hope to reap aria applause, and in which the claque cannot even earn their supper.

I would ask the producers when distributing the parts to disregard all demands of the primadonna assoluta or the first baritone. Just as the actors in this opera *Intermezzo* are not operatic heroes but should represent genuine human beings, the casting of the singers for *Intermezzo* should be governed by any existing talent for a light conversational tone, and by musical and physical aptitude for the characters to be portrayed.

The producer should ensure that the actors learn to master the purely musical part during piano-rehearsals to such an extent that they are completely independent of the conductor's baton during the stage rehearsal and especially during the first orchestral rehearsal, and can therefore devote all their energy to the natural presentation of this modern conversation piece.

For the benefit of the conductor I would add in conclusion that the metronome figures I have given in this opera, as in others, refer to ideal metronomes, and may therefore be modified at liberty in order to enable the singer to attain an unimpeded, clear pronunciation of the text according to his vocal and musical qualities, and in order to allow for the size and acoustic properties of the theatre and the distance between actor and listener.

By turning its back upon the popular love-and-murder interest of the usual operatic libretto, and by taking its subject-matter perhaps too exclusively from real life, this new work blazes a path for musical and dramatic composition which others after me may perhaps negotiate with more talent and better fortune. I am fully aware of the fact that in breaking new ground unthought-of difficulties will stand in the way of the correct realisation of my intentions. May this preface assist and guide the worthy and generous interpreters of my art, the excellent singers and hard-working conductors, in the solution of these problems.

[Garmisch, 28th June, 1924]

INTERVIEW ON *DIE AEGYPTISCHE HELENA*

YOU wish me to say a few words about *Die Aegyptische Helena?* There is little I can say about the music; it is, I am afraid, melodious and tuneful and unfortunately does not present any problem to ears which belong to the 20th century. Problems— the word has become the popular slogan of eternal adolescents and is always connected with works which fall short of being master- pieces. In Mozart for example, there are no problems. One could almost say that in Mozart problems are resolved before they have even been posed. Apart from this, the music tries to adopt a noble Greek posture similar to that of Goethe's *Iphigenia.*

As far as the text is concerned, I hope it will not present to readers and critics the difficulties which curiously enough have been encountered in *Die Frau ohne Schatten.* In my opinion it would not have been very difficult to interpret aright certain symbols in that opera, even if they might be out of the ordinary. There is always the danger that operatic libretti will be criticised before the music which goes with the text has been heard, so that we can say that only he who is capable of composing the music is in a position to assess its value from the start. I have often won- dered whether any composer of the last century would have con- sidered it possible for the libretto of *Die Meistersinger*, with the exception of Walter's three songs, to be set to music at all. But in the meantime you have read the libretto and would, I under- stand, like to put a few questions to me.

What were Hofmannsthal's sources?

Very few. The only relevant passage occurs in the fourth book of the Odyssey where, on the occasion of Telemachus' visit to Sparta, Helen, the divine daughter of Chronos, mixes a drink in the presence of her long since reconciled husband, which has the power of robbing grief and anger of their sting and of banishing all painful memories. According to Homer, Helen gives this drink, called Lethe, to her husband Menelaus whenever Troy is mentioned. This is the ancient story which Hofmannsthal takes up. He makes the second main female character in the opera, the nymph Aithra, offer to husband and wife a brew of Lotus leaves and she gives them the potion to take with them into the solitude of the desert, so that Helen may from time to time slip Lotus, the magic herb of forgetfulness, into her husband's cup.

But I do not think there is any need to remind a well-read public that potions of oblivion and of remembrance were not invented by Homer, just as the potion of death and love in *Tristan* was not invented by Richard Wagner. They belong to the age-old stock-in-trade of the poet for the concentration of dramatic situations and are found even before the days of Homer and the Edda in the oldest Indian, Celtic and Teutonic legends.

I consider it to be one of the most attractive ideas in Hofmannsthal's text that Helen is not satisfied to regain her husband's affection with the aid of the potion of oblivion and of a story cleverly constructed by the nymph Aithra, but that she should, after renewed tragic doubts and experiences, insist, in the second act, on winning through on her own strength, in spite of and without the aid of magic potions, solely by the divine power of beauty and by her own dynamic nature.

In the Easter number of the Neue Freie Presse *I read that Hofmannsthal also bases his story on Euripides. What truth is there in this?*

The idea of the 'spectre' which the Gods are said to have sent to Troy to destroy the Trojans instead of the real Helen, whilst the real Helen was preserved for Menelaus' return after the war, is taken from Euripides' *Helena*. But this motif is only touched upon lightly. It serves as a basis for the story by means of which Aithra seeks to save Helen.

All the essentials are therefore Hofmannsthal's invention?

Yes. And it is curious that this psychologically most interesting subject should never have been used by a poet for so many thousands of years. We had nothing to go on, apart from the few passages mentioned above, according to which Menelaus and Helen lived together reunited in Sparta after the Trojan war. The psychological developments which led to this reconciliation form the content of Hofmannsthal's text and they presented a very gratifying task to the composer. This is the first time that the human tragedy of *Helena in Egypt* has been dramatically presented, since Goethe's Helen in the second part of *Faust* is mainly a symbol of the ancient world, as proverbially the most beautiful woman of Greek legend, and Goethe evades the real solution of the conflict by whisking Helen away from her native sphere to Faust's castle. I only hope that this dangerous Helen, who provoked the deadly Trojan war and who caused me much annoyance before her rebirth may bestow some of the delights which, according to legend, it is in her power to give, on the two authors of this opera, who have attempted to interpret her fate after the Trojan war.

[1928]

PREFACE TO *CAPRICCIO*

Motto: '*Der Arie ihr Recht!*
Auf die Sänger nimm Rücksicht!
Nicht zu laut das Orchester . . .'
(Give the aria its due!
Be considerate to the singers!
Let the orchestra be subdued)
La Roche, Der Theaterdirektor.

WHEN he has obeyed this maxim of his teacher, the average theatre conductor is satisfied that he has done his duty towards the individuals whose vocation it is to maintain as best they can the claims of the human voice against the inexorable arm of the sergeant-major of the baton and his orchestra wallowing in *mezzo forte* playing. 'One could hear the singers very well to-night and could even follow the text here and there . . .' This is a phrase of which the ruling *Musical Director* is always particularly proud. And rightly so, for does it not represent a considerable step forward on the road towards a decent performance of opera?—nor, apart from guessing at the right tempi, is it at all easy for a conductor in the midst of the orchestra, surrounded by anything from thirty-four to sixty-four strings which he considers it his duty at all times to subdue whilst the brass, sitting farther away from him (and even the woodwind), are the real murderers of the singers, to find the proper balance between the stage and his 'symphonic accompaniment', a balance which not only dress-circle and stalls but also the galleries are justified in demanding.

The patron-saint of this theoretical comedy, the idea of which was first suggested by the title of a long-forgotten operatic libretto by the Abbé de Casti: '*Prima le Parole, dopo la musica*', namely Gluck, the great reformer of the style of composition,

wrote a preface to his *Alceste* which determined for a whole
century the development of music drama. May I, who stand at
the end of this development, be allowed, after fifty years of conducting experience to add, by way of an epilogue, some little
advice with particular reference to this opera *Capriccio* which
may benefit those of my colleagues of the rostrum who take the
trouble to give serious study to my operatic scores. In view of the
great diligence with which conductors, solo repetiteurs and singers on all operatic stages devote themselves to musical studies, and
considering the importance given to the spoken word in this
particular work, it would not seem inopportune to suggest that,
before study of the score begins, the producer should arrange a few
through reading rehearsals (solely based on the text) with special
emphasis on the clearest possible pronunciation of consonants: e.g.
of the letters at the beginning and the end of words—readings
which should moreover be repeated without any music before the
last stage rehearsals (from two to three days before the dress
rehearsal).

As far as the orchestral score is concerned, I need hardly mention today that there must be a number of thorough rehearsals for
strings, woodwind and brass alone. But it is particularly profitable
to carry out rehearsals for the whole orchestra so thoroughly that
detailed adjustments in the playing of individual groups and of
individual instruments in the orchestra are no longer necessary
when the singers join the rehearsal. At this point I would suggest
that, after a few stage rehearsals, the conductor should entrust
his baton to a colleague who is also familiar with the work and
should himself spend several rehearsals listening from different
positions in the house to the whole body of sound of which, no
matter how great his ability and how good his ear, he will never
be able to gain an entirely accurate impression from his rostrum.
Before describing the last phase of the rehearsals for my operas,
I would like to stray a little farther afield.

There can be no doubt that the homophonous accompanying orchestra of the early and middle-aged Verdi (which this great master even then handled with particular delicacy and a great wealth of invention) is the dearest companion to the singer as he finds his way to the heart of a public clamouring for an *encore*.

Recitativo secco (interrupted only by chords played by the strings and the cembalo) is the most primitive musical form in which a fairly complicated comic action can be clearly expressed.

The trouble starts as soon as there is a single voice in the orchestra raised against it. In Mozart, arias, duets, quartets are no longer purely lyrical outpourings during which the action is arrested but (not to mention his inspired finales) they are filled to bursting-point with a dramatic life of their own which carries on the action, and already in *Figaro* and *Così fan tutte* there are contrapuntal passages in the orchestra where quickly declaiming vocal parts have difficulty in speeding words to the upper galleries against the combined effort of sustained woodwind, high horns, and *figured* string quartet.

It is in Richard Wagner's work that we find the ideal relationship between vocal parts and orchestra. Verses forged from the purest gold of the German language, phrased with the subtlest feeling for word-derivation and formed into the most expressive of vocal lines are, in the masterly alternation of *recitativo* and *cantilena* and in the most beautifully articulated melodies both on the stage and in the orchestra—guided and supported by an orchestra which explains and excites by its use of motifs and sculptural subtlety and by its polyphony which is never superfluous—made the content of profound and edifying works in which we find a correct assessment of the distance from the stage to the listener paralleled only in Schiller's dramatic poems.

May I, fully conscious though I am that Wagner's work is a unique miracle in its perfection, venture in connection with the suggestions for performances of my own dramatic works given above, to point to a peculiarity of their style which, unless carefully observed will introduce much obscurity into their performance, and may even produce misunderstandings for which, as their author, I alone would not be held responsible. I know only too well that my orchestra, high-pitched as it frequently is, presents more difficulties to the singers than the dark velvet carpet of a Wagnerian string quintet, and that a flute playing independently above the soprano part is sufficient to detract from the comprehensibility of the text—I know only too well that the clear exposition on the one hand of the countless ramifications of my polyphony and the necessity on the other hand of subduing this when accompanying the singers, present a difficult task to the conductor; it is therefore all the more important to pay the greatest possible attention to the control of the relationship between voice and orchestra as suggested above.

I know of cases where a solo violin (Mozart aria, first scene of *Daphne*) can hardly hold its own against a singer whose tone is too big, whereas on the other hand strings and woodwind, when scored a little higher than a soprano passage in the middle register, can completely drown the latter even when playing *pp*. How often must not a balance be established from bar to bar at a moment's notice by the conductor as well as by the singer, by allowing the one or the other element to protrude or to recede if the sound picture envisaged by the composer is to be realised, i.e. if the main theme, distributed over the different groups and individual instruments, is to be merged into one melody together with the vocal part.

In accordance with the above remarks special attention should be given to each '*espressivo*' marked in the orchestral parts.

When *Die Walküre* was rehearsed seventy years ago in Munich, my old piano teacher, the harpist Tombo, asked Richard Wagner what he was to do with the harp part of the *Feuerzauber*: It was unplayable. Wagner replied 'I am not a harpist.' You see what I mean. It is your task to arrange the part in such a way that it sounds as I want it.' This applies more or less to all performances of opera. Opera houses vary in size and acoustic qualities. Voices differ in quality and power.

Orchestras differ in composition (the string quartet is almost invariably too weak). Felix Mottl, who had for years applied in vain for an increase of the first violins from ten to twelve, once said to me sadly; 'With less than ten first violins, it's all chamber music'.

'The score tells you exactly how I want it.' The task of conductor and producer in realising such a libretto and such a score in accordance with the author's intentions is so great and manifold that it cannot be appreciated enough by the audience and the critic when a performance is completely successful.

A faithful interpretation of music and words alike and congenial improvisation are 'brother and sister', just like word and sound.

Vienna, 7th April, 1942.

SOME GOOD PROGRAMMES OF MY WORKS

Couperin-Suite
Also sprach Zarathustra
Symphonia Domestica

Don Quixote
Ein Heldenleben

Bourgeois Gentilhomme Suite
2nd Horn Concerto
Macbeth
Don Juan
Death and Transfiguration

Aus Italien
Eine Alpensinfonie
Festliches Praeludium

Light programme:
Divertimento
'Schlagobers'-Suite
Waltz and reverie from 'Intermezzo'
Potpourri-Overture to 'Die schweigsame Frau'
Till Eulenspiegel

[1941]

ON INSPIRATION IN MUSIC

MELODY as revealed in the greatest works of our classics and up to Richard Wagner, is one of the most noble gifts which an invisible deity has bestowed on mankind.

Mozart's melodies, the G minor string quintet, Beethoven's symphonies, sonatas, and quartets (A flat major adagio of the E flat major quartet, opus 127), Schubert's songs, acts two and three of *Tristan* (to mention only a few outstanding masterpieces) are symbols in which are revealed the most profound spiritual truths, and they are not 'invented', but are 'given in their dreams' to those privileged to receive them. Whence they come no one knows, not even their creator, the unconscious mouthpiece of the demiurge.

The melodic idea which suddenly falls upon me out of the blue, which emerges without the prompting of an external sensual stimulant or of some spiritual emotion—the latter, by the way, can be a direct cause more than anything else, as I have often experienced after excitements of a completely different nature entirely unconnected with art—appears in the imagination immediately, unconsciously, uninfluenced by reason. It is the greatest gift of the divinity and cannot be compared with anything else.

Poetic inspiration may be somehow connected with the intellect if only because it must express itself in words—musical inspiration is the absolute revelation of innermost secrets. That is why Goethe's famous remark made to Eckermann on May 6th, 1827: 'My mind received impressions, impressions moreover of a sensual, vital, amiable, colourful, varied nature, such as a vivid imagination presented to me; and all I had to do as a poet was to fashion such perceptions and impressions artistically within myself and to present them by lively description in such a way that others might receive the same impressions when reading or hearing what I wrote', covers only a part of the poet's activity and the purely mechanical part at that. *Inspiration* itself and especially musical inspiration in melody, is not even touched by it. Goethe's words are a very modest formulation of the poet's activity and, purely accidentally, were probably designed merely for Eckermann's intellectual capacity: they are not exhaustive, nor do they touch the essence of the work of the artistic imagination.

Nor is that other sentence of Goethe's: 'I have always considered all my work and achievement as symbolical', any more than a paraphrase of that unconscious creative urge manifested in its purest and most immediate form in melodic inspiration, in so far as it is really 'inspiration' without any co-operation on the part of the intellect.

What is 'the soul'? Where is the seat of the imagination? Is the latter a higher form of reason, the highest flower of the human soul? Has fancy taken its seat in the brain and does it only operate when fructified by the blood? To judge from my own experience, which is that my artistic imagination is particularly stimulated by excitement and annoyance—and not, as is frequently supposed, by sensual impressions, by the beauty of nature, or by solemn moods evoked by poetic landscapes (such impressions are more easily translated into sound pictures by the working of the mind i.e. at one remove, not directly), I am almost inclined to believe that the human blood contains chemical elements which, when flowing through certain nerves or when coming into contact with certain parts of the brain, cause this highest stimulation of spiritual and mental activity which produced the masterpieces of art. The birth of melody represents the culmination of such activity. The fact that such ideas very frequently occur to one on awakening in the morning, at the moment when the brain, emptied of blood during the night, begins to be replenished with fresh blood, would seem to indicate that the blood has a greater influence on the activity of the imagination than purely mental work.

Brain, nerves, blood—which is the strongest factor?

What is inspiration? Generally speaking we understand by musical inspiration the invention of a motif, a melody which occurs to one suddenly, unsolicited by the intellect, especially immediately after awakening in the early morning or in dreams, —Sachs's words in the *Meistersinger: 'Glaubt mir des Menschen wahrster Wahn wird ihm im Traume aufgetan'*. (Man's truest intuition is revealed to him in dreams.) Am I to believe that my imagination has been at work all night independently of consciousness and without recollection in the platonic sense?

My own experience has been this: If I am held up at a certain point in my composition at night and cannot see a profitable way of continuing in spite of much deliberation, I close the lid of the piano or the cover of my manuscript book and go to bed, and when I wake up in the morning—lo and behold! I have found the continuation. By what mental or physical process is this brought about?

Or should I, in accordance with common parlance, call musical inspiration whatever is so new and fascinating, so compelling and penetrating 'to the depths of the heart' (Leonore), that it cannot be compared with anything that has gone before? Quality? From where do they come, the indescribable melodies of our classics (Haydn, Mozart, Beethoven, Schubert), for which there are no prototypes? Not even in Johann Sebastian Bach's adagio movements, nor in the works of his son Philip Emanuel can be found more than the intimations of melodies which would bear comparison with Mozart's vast and infinite melodies—not only in the arias of his operas but also in his instrumental works (only to mention his G minor string quintet). But how much in these divine creations is immediate inspiration, or primary invention, and how much is due to the operation of the mind? Where is the dividing line between the activity of the mind and that of the imagination?

In the case of our classic composers it is particularly difficult to decide this question. Such is the wealth of their melodies and the originality of the melodies themselves, so new and yet so different from each other, that it is difficult to draw the line between the first immediate inspiration and its continuation and expansion into the finished extended vocal phrases. This applies particularly to Mozart and Schubert, who left this world in early manhood and yet created work of such immensity. (My father used to say: What Mozart wrote in his thirty-six years, i.e. what he composed, the best copyist could not write out in that time.) It must have been dictated into an inspired pen by angels, as Pfitzner describes it so beautifully in the final scene of the first act of *Palestrina*. There can be no question here of work such as can be found in Beethoven's sketchbooks. Everything seems to be immediate inspiration.

To judge from my own experience of creative work, a motif or a melodic phrase of two or four bars occurs to me immediately. I put this down on paper and then expand it straight away into a phrase of eight, sixteen or thirty-two bars which is not of course left unaltered, but after a longer or shorter period of 'rest' is slowly fashioned into its final form, which must hold its own against the severest and most detached self-criticism. Now this operation is carried out in such a manner that what is most important is to wait for the moment when the imagination is willing and ready to serve me further. But this state of preparation is usually produced and stimulated at leisure, after continued thought, and even, as I remarked above, by spiritual excitement (even indignation and annoyance). These mental processes do not belong solely to the sphere of innate talent but also to those of self-criticism and self-education. Goethe is supposed to have said 'Genius is industry', but even industry and joy in one's work are innate and not only the results of training. A perfect work of art is achieved only when, as in the case of our great masters, content and form are blended to perfection.

Our musicologists—I would mention the two greatest names: Friedrich von Hausegger (*Music as Expression*) and Eduard Hanslick (*Music as Form Moving in Sound*)—have given definitions which have since been considered incompatible. This is wrong. These are the two mutually complementary forms of musical creation. The starting-points of modern music are of different kinds. Form moving in sound originates, I suppose, in the dance—music as expression, on the other hand, originates in the cry of pain and in the desire to give artistic form to religious adoration (in the Gregorian chant, in Palestrina's masses and in J. S. Bach's chorales). Simultaneously starting with Monteverdi, the *recitativo* was developed, which was eventually turned into the aria, and with it, into the modern opera.

We can call 'form moving in sound' most of the allegro movements in Bach's and Handel's intrumental works, in the slow movements of which a more profound emotion is already struggling for expression—an emotion which was later to speak immediately to our hearts in the works of Haydn, Mozart, Beethoven, Schubert, running the gamut of the emotions with a formally perfected logic. The so-called sonata form, which from Haydn to Beethoven's last works became so completely one with the emotional content of the music, has not been achieved since by any of the successors of these heroes, e.g. by Brahms or Bruckner, in whose workmanlike compositions sonata form became a conventional formula, within which we became painfully conscious again and again of deliberate music-making whereas, when listening to a Haydn quartet, we cannot help opening mouth and ears wide with delight.

I suppose we can call these instrumental works of the classics 'form moving in sound' also, but they are no longer a rhythmically moving play of sounds, as in Bach and Handel, but have become the expression of the noblest emotions of the soul coloured by joy or passion. In the variation form, which is popular to this day and finally became somewhat barren (in my *Don Quixote* I carried it *ad absurdum* and parodied it tragicomically), we find united the whole of the figured material invented and increasingly enriched by the classics. Richard Wagner at last put all kinds of figured material, together with the most emotional vocal melodic line, into the service of dramatic expression. *Tristan, Der Ring des Nibelungen, Die Meistersinger, Parsifal*, form the zenith which all the various manifestations of 'form moving in sound' and of 'Musical expression' endeavoured to attain. With Wagner, music reached its greatest capacity of expression.

[*ca.* 1940]

REMINISCENCES OF HANS VON BÜLOW

TO anyone who ever heard him play Beethoven or conduct Wagner, or who ever attended his music lessons or listened to him during orchestral rehearsals, he was bound to be the example of all the shining virtues of the reproductive artist. The touching interest he took in me and his influence on the development of my artistic talent were, apart from my friendship with Alexander Ritter, who to my father's grief made a Wagnerian of me, the most decisive factors in my career. Whatever feeling for the art of interpretation I can call my own I owe, apart from my father (whom Bülow used to call 'the Joachim of the horn') to my father's determined opponent, Hans von Bülow. Not that these two men hated each other like enemies on the field of battle: on the contrary, when they played together harmony reigned supreme. My father played the *cantilenas* of *Die Meistersinger* and of *Tristan* so beautifully that, as he himself told me with a smile of satisfaction, even Wagner had to confess: 'Old Strauss is an unbearable fellow, but when he plays his horn one cannot be cross with him'. And Bülow on the other hand was so well-versed in *Tristan*—although at that time, in Munich, he lacked the routine of an operatic conductor—that even my father obeyed the whims of his baton when, with fire and sword, i.e. with endless rehearsals and north German asperity, he drummed his beloved Wagner into the Munich orchestra, used as it was only to the Bavarian rudeness of the old Franz Lachner. It was not until the music was over that the heated spirits joined battle and the mixture of mutual admiration and diametrically opposed opinions on music determined the curious course of the relationship between these two men.

Thus it happened that Bülow in his magnanimity took the first opportunity of heaping coals of fire upon the head of the hated old Strauss when my first publisher, Bülow's friend Eugen Spitzweg, sent to the leader of the Meiningen orchestra my Serenade for Woodwind, Opus 7. He incorporated the piece, which is nothing more than the respectable work of a music student, into his touring repertoire. It was on the occasion of one such performance in Berlin in the winter of 1883 that I made his acquaintance. He commissioned me to write a similar piece for the Meiningen orchestra. I went to work immediately (happy days of my youth, when I could still work to order) and sent him, during that summer, my Suite for Woodwind in B flat major, in four movements. In the winter of 1884 Bülow came to Munich and surprised me, when I visited him, by informing me that he would give a matinée performance before an invited audience, after the third official concert, the programme of which was to contain as its second item my Suite for Woodwind, which I was to conduct. I thanked him, overjoyed, but told him that I had never had a baton in my hand before and asked him when I could rehearse. 'There will be no rehearsals, the orchestra has no time for such things on tour'. His order was so categorical that I had no time to ponder over my discomfiture. The morning of the day arrived. I went to fetch Bülow at his hotel; he was in a dreadful mood. As we went up the steps of the Odeon, he positively raved against Munich, which had driven out Wagner and himself, and against old Perfall; he called the Odeon a cross between a church and a stock exchange, in short, he was as charmingly unbearable as he could only be when he was furious about something. The matinée took its course. I conducted my piece in a state of slight coma; I can only remember to-day that I made no blunders. What it was like, apart from that, I could not say. Bülow did not even listen to my debut; smoking one cigarette after another, he paced furiously up and down in the music room. When I went in, my father, profoundly moved, came in through the opposite door in order to thank Bülow.

That was what Bülow had been waiting for: like a furious lion he pounced upon my father: 'You have nothing to thank me for', he shouted, 'I have not forgotten what you have done to me in this damned city of Munich. What I did to-day I did because your son has talent and not for you.' Without saying a word my father left the music-room, from which all the others had long since fled when they saw Bülow explode. This scene had, of course, thoroughly spoiled my debut for me. Only Bülow was suddenly in the best of spirits. Later, Bülow more than made up to my father for the injury he had done him and my father bore no grudge against his son's benefactor. A short time afterwards, Bülow appointed me second conductor in Meiningen as successor to Mannstaedt, thus opening a career which started under his auspices and was to be favoured by fortune.

On the first of October 1885 I embarked in my new post upon an apprenticeship which could hardly have been more interesting, impressive and—amusing. Every day, from nine o'clock until noon, were held the memorable rehearsals such as Bülow alone could conduct. Ever since that time the memory of the works he then conducted, all of them by heart, has never been effaced for me. In particular, I found the way in which he brought out the poetic content of Beethoven's and Wagner's works absolutely convincing. There was no trace anywhere of arbitrariness. Everything was of compelling necessity, born of the form and content of the work itself; his captivating temperament, governed always by the strictest artistic discipline, and his loyalty to the spirit and the letter of the work of art (these two are more akin than is commonly believed) ensured that by dint of painstaking rehearsals these works were performed with a clarity which constitutes to me to this day the zenith of perfection in the performance of orchestral works. The gracefulness with which he handled the baton, the charming manner in which he used to conduct his rehearsals—instruction frequently taking

the form of a witty epigram—are unforgettable; when he suddenly turned away from the rostrum and put a question to the
pupil reading the score, the latter had to answer quickly if he
were not to be taunted with a sarcastic remark by the master in
front of the assembled orchestra. He was the wittiest compère
who ever adopted the guise of a schoolmaster of genius. As a
pedagogue he could be relentlessly pedantic and his motto:
'Learn to read the score of a Beethoven symphony *accurately*
first, and you will have found its interpretation,' would be an
adornment to the main door of any conservatoire to this day.
He hated all nonchalance in matters of art. I should like to give
an example of this: at his invitation I conducted my *Macbeth* in
Berlin in 1892 and Bülow attended the rehearsal. I myself had
not looked at the piece for a long time and (always a little careless
in that respect, as I used to rely on my reasonable skill in reading
scores) had not looked at the score even before the rehearsal, so
that the members of the Philharmonic Orchestra witnessed the
spectacle of a composer glued to the notes of his score. This
annoyed the conscientious Bülow, and afterwards he reproached
me bitterly: 'You should have the score in your head and not
your head in the score', and (anticipating my rejoinder), 'even if
you have composed the thing yourself'. It was at the same rehearsal that Bülow remarked upon a printing error in the second
horn part of the Breitkopf edition of a Beethoven symphony. A
famous critic who had been admitted to the rehearsal rushed up
to Bülow full of enthusiasm after the rehearsal and asked him to
show him the interesting printing error once more. Bülow
opened the score at any old page and pointed at random to a
passage in the horn part: 'There it is'.—'Quite right, of course,
of course' confirmed the critic. Bülow, who had rightly assumed
that the critic's knowledge did not extend to transposing horn
parts, registered the discomfiture of 'this authority on Music'
with a sarcastic smile. But one could go on telling such stories

forever. There was, for example, the double performance of the Ninth Symphony in Berlin to which I had come especially from Munich with Alexander von Ritter. When we first called on Bülow in his room we met Johannes Brahms there, whom Bülow once again introduced with the words: 'You have come to hear the Ninth Symphony? Meet the composer of the tenth'. I can still see the furious face of Ritter, who was a fanatical admirer of Liszt. Brahms too was a little embarrassed. Later he was to remark: 'Hans von Bülow's praise smarts like salt in the eyes so that the tears run.' I would not doubt for a minute that Bülow with his artistic acumen sincerely admired Brahms's achievements. But the following experience does, I think, illustrate clearly on which side his sympathies really lay. During a popular concert given by the Philharmonic Orchestra Bülow had conducted the *Tannhäuser* overture in the self-possessed and captivating manner which was his very own. But his childhood friend and school-mate Ritter, who had heard the overture played in Dresden in the forties under Wagner himself, together with Bülow, who had always valued his judgment, had not given him a word of praise. The next morning they passed each other on the hotel stairs. Bülow rushed up to Ritter and asked 'How did you like the *Tannhäuser* overture yesterday?', and the stubborn old man replied: 'Oh, it was indescribably wonderful. It reminded me vividly of the time when we both worshipped an ideal to which *I* have remained faithful.' Whereupon Bülow embraced his friend with tears streaming from his eyes and ran upstairs to his room without saying a word.

To return to the October of 1885: in the course of a fortnight of daily rehearsals under Bülow I had acquired a good grounding in conductorship, at last in theory, when Bülow informed me that he was going away for a day and that I would have to rehearse Brahms's A major serenade with the orchestra. I was conducting busily when the Princess arrived with her train to attend the rehearsal. I was sufficiently versed in court manners to interrupt the rehearsal and to ask Her Highness what were her orders. She replied: 'I would like to hear the overture to *The Flying Dutchman.*' This meant renewed embarrassment for me. It was my second time at the rostrum and I had never looked at the score of the overture of the *Dutchman* before. With all the bashfulness of my twenty years I replied: 'But I have never conducted the overture of *The Flying Dutchman.*' The Princess, who may well have thought, 'What a conductor!' said ironically: 'Well, I hope you know the *Freischütz* overture'. At this point I pulled myself together and replied: 'In that case I'd rather play the overture of *The Flying Dutchman*, and it went off quite well because the orchestra knew the work and I beat time with the courage of desperation. My public debut followed a week later. Bülow wanted me to play Mozart's Pianoforte Concerto in C Minor. Although I had practised busily all summer, the idea of playing the concerto with Bülow conducting filled me—by no means a fully-trained pianist—with fear and trembling. When we had negotiated the first movement quite creditably, the master encouraged me with the words, 'If you weren't something better, you might become a pianist.' Although I did not think that I fully deserved this compliment, my self-confidence had been increased sufficiently to enable me to play the last two movements a little less self-consciously. After this, I conducted my F minor symphony. No less a man than Johannes Brahms was in the audience and I was very anxious to hear his criticism. In his laconic manner he said to me 'Quite nice', but then added the following memorable piece of advice: 'Take a good look at Schubert's dances, young man, and try your luck at the invention of simple eight-bar melodies.' I owe it mainly to Johannes Brahms that I have never since refrained from incorporating a popular melody in my work, although our dogmatic critics to-day think little of such melodies. They only occur to one on rare occasions

and at happy moments. I also remember clearly a further criticism made by the great master: 'Your symphony is too full of
thematic irrelevancies. There is no point in this piling up of many
themes which are only contrasted rhythmically on one triad.' It
was then that I realised that counterpoint is only justified when
poetic necessity compels a temporary union of two or several
themes contrasted as sharply as possible, not only rhythmically
but especially harmonically. The most shining example of this
sort of poetic counterpoint is found in the third act of *Tristan und
Isolde*.

A few days after this, Brahms's Fourth Symphony was first
performed. Bülow rehearsals were outstanding and his enthusiasm and touching conscientiousness had often contrasted
strangely with the indifference which Brahms himself manifested towards the dynamics and the presentation of his work.

The concert was concluded with the *Academic Festival Overture* in which, in order to pay homage to Brahms personally (and
to avoid reducing even further the number of the few strings of
the Meiningen orchestra), Bülow undertook to play the cymbals
and I the big drum, but it transpired that neither of us could
count rests. During the rehearsal I lost count after the fourth
bar and eventually helped myself by putting a score on my desk.
Bülow on the other hand, whose attention constantly wandered
from his part which also consisted mainly of rests, invariably
stopped after eight bars of steady counting and kept running to
the trumpeter to ask: 'To what letter have we got?' and then he
would start afresh: 'One, two, three, four.' I do not think a
greater mess has ever been made of the percussion parts than on
the evening when the two conductors took a hand.

To conclude this informal chat, here are a few amusing inci-
dents which occurred during Bülow's rehearsals. Reliable as the
master's memory usually was, even he made a mistake every
now and then. Once he suddenly rushed up to the first horn

player and poured upon him a flood of abuse. Now it was policy in the Meiningen orchestra not to say a word when the beloved master was furious, but just to let him rave until he had finished. When Bülow had finished and was taking a breath, the horn player said quietly: 'But sir, it was not I at all, that passage is in the third horn.' At this even Bülow had to laugh and the rehearsal was completed in unruffled harmony. On another occasion Bülow was in the midst of Berlioz' *Harold* symphony when Duke George entered the theatre, followed by his adjutant, Herr von Kotze. Bülow immediately broke off and asked what where the Duke's wishes. The affable Duke only wanted to listen and asked what was being played. Berlioz' symphony, replied Bülow, but added that he was unable to play the work for the Duke because he had only just begun to rehease it. The Duke replied: 'Never mind, I'll just listen'. Bülow: 'I am very sorry, Sir, the performance is not polished enough; I cannot play it for Your Highness.' The Duke then said: ' But Bülow, don't be funny. It does not matter how it is played, I shall be glad to listen'. Bülow, bowing stiffly for the third time: 'I am really sorry. At the stage we have reached with the symphony it would do, at the most, for Herr von Kotze.' On the stage, the grinning orchestra; in the centre, Bülow in impeccable court attitude; below them the Duke and the poor victim. It made a pretty picture.

My apprenticeship in Meiningen came to an end on the 1st of April, 1886. After the conflict with Brahms over the performance of the E minor symphony in Frankfrot-on-Main, Bülow had handed in his resignation the previous November; I accepted a call to Munich after four months during which, as sole ruler over the orchestra, I had played and rehearsed in daily rehearsals everything there was to be played in concert literature. It was during this winter that the famous Meiningen theatre did not go on tour and I did not, of course, miss a single one of the

wonderful performances. When I said good-bye to the Ducal
family, Frau von Heldburg, who had always been a little
jealous of Bülow and the fame of the orchestra, made the following gracious farewell remark: 'The Duke and I regret to lose
you so soon (I was just about to make my first gratified bow),
you were—the best cheer-leader we've had in our theatre for a
very long time.'

[1910]

REMINISCENCES OF MY FATHER

MY father was born in the Oberpfalz on the basalt fortress of Parkstein, near Weiden, and was the son of a warder of the castle. I suspect, from his facial characteristics which, with his high forehead and hooked nose, were somewhat reminiscent of a Circassian chieftain (his figure was tall and lean), that he was of Bohemian origin, but I have no direct proof of this. He was what is called a man of principle. He would have considered it dishonest ever to revise a judgment on an artistic subject once he had arrived at it, and remained impervious to my theories even in his old age. His musical creed worshipped the trinity of Mozart (above the others), Haydn and Beethoven. These were followed by the Lieder composer Schubert, by Weber, and, at some distance, by Mendelssohn and Spohr.

To him the later Beethoven works, from the finale of the seventh symphony onward, were no longer 'pure music' (one could almost scent in them that mephistophelian figure, Richard Wagner). He approved of Schumann's compositions for the piano up to op. 20; his later compositions, on the other hand, because they were influenced by Mendelssohn and because of their rhythmic monotonies and repetition of phrases, were labelled 'Leipzig music' and were accordingly valued less highly. (Compare the interesting rhythm of the 6/8 theme in the first movement of Beethoven's seventh symphony and the difference is obvious). Where music ceased to be a play of sounds and became, quite consciously, music as expression, my father only followed with mental reservations. He approved of *Tannhäuser; Lohengrin* was too sweet for his liking and he was incapable of appreciating the later Wagner, although no one gave as spirited a rendering of the horn solo in *Tristan* and *Die Meistersinger* as he. He commanded a magnificent full tone and improvised like

Bülow, who admired him greatly, although in questions of music they never saw eye to eye with each other. In the controversial days of the first performances of *Tristan* and *Die Meistersinger*, feeling ran high. Bülow rehearsed relentlessly. At the end of an interminable *Meistersinger* rehearsal, my father was 'cracking' on practically every note. Bülow kept on interrupting. At last my father said: 'I can't go on', whereupon Bülow snapped: 'Then why don't you retire?' Wagner once went past the horn player, who was sitting at his place in the orchestra in moody silence, and said, 'Always gloomy, these horn players', whereupon my father replied: 'We have good reason to be'. He declared that the horn parts of *Die Meistersinger* were really clarinet parts, notwithstanding which he played them so beautifully that Wagner payed him the compliment of saying: 'Strauss is an unbearable fellow, but when he plays his horn, one cannot be cross with him.' Once, Wagner, standing on the stage, had such an argument with my father, in the orchestra pit, that words failed Wagner in his fury and he left in high dudgeon, whereupon my father triumphantly commented: 'I have put him to flight'. After the first *Tristan* rehearsal in the small Residenz Theatre my father met Cosima, Bülow and Wagner at Halbreiter's, the music publishers. Wagner, still under the spell of the rehearsal, exclaimed: 'First *Tristan* rehearsal! Sounded wonderful!' My father replied: 'I don't agree. In that small theatre with its rotten acoustics it sounded as if it were in an old saucepan.' Wagner replied furiously: 'Not at all, it sounded wonderful.' The last encounter of the two opponents took place in 1882 at Bayreuth, where my father, to please Hermann Levi, was playing in *Parsifal*. Before one of the rehearsals he addressed the Munich Court Orchestra of which he was the spokesman, to say that at the request of many members of the orchestra he had arranged for a communal lunch in the Bürgerverein at the price of one Mark. At this moment Wagner appeared on the bridge above the orchestra and immediately interrupted my father with the words: 'But I have made special arrangements for a communal luncheon in the theatre restaurant.' My father: 'That does not suit the members of our orchestra. They prefer to go home after the rehearsal and to eat in the town'.—'Then eat your sour gherkins where you please'. These were the last words the great master addressed to his old opponent, who played under him once more, however, when Richard Wagner personally conducted the final scene of the third act of *Parsifal* during the last performance in 1882. On the 13th of February, of the following year he closed his eyes for the last time in an ungrateful Germany.

With Bülow, on the other hand, my father remained on friendly terms even after Bülow's departure, in spite of the fact that they did not see eye to eye with each other on questions of music. Bülow himself told me that, a year after his departure from Munich, he went to his old Munich barber for a shave on the way through, whereupon the barber welcomed him with the words: 'Aren't you ever going to come back to us, Herr von Bülow?' Bülow replied: 'No, not to this damned hole.' 'It's your own fault, Herr von Bülow, you should never have said 'thirty swine more or less'; the people of Munich cannot stand the Prussian word 'swine'. If you had said: 'It does not matter a hoot whether thirty rotten big-wigs more or less sit there' when the row of stalls was taken out of the Hoftheater, nobody would have minded.'

My father was very quick-tempered. It was always a somewhat exhausting pleasure to play with him. He had an infallible feeling for the right tempo. He criticised his chief, Hermann Levi, on the grounds that he never found the right tempo before the third bar of a piece. He believed in strict rhythm. How often did he not shout at me: 'Why this Jewish haste?' But I learned how to play well when I accompanied him time and time again in Mozart's beautiful horn concertos and in Beethoven's horn sonatas. He gave me a worthy preparation for the *haute école* of playing and for Bülow's interpretation of classical masterpieces, when in the July of 1885 I attended the latter's series of lectures on Beethoven's pianoforte works at the Raff Conservatoire in Frankfort, and witnessed in October of that year the daily rehearsals for the entire repertory of the Meiningen Court Orchestra. Bülow conducted even rehearsals by heart, but gave me the scores and frequently interrupted the rehearsals with advice, and addressed searchingly tricky questions to me.

When my father played in opera and concerts, he always regarded it as a solemn act. He spent weeks preparing for the difficult horn soli of Beethoven's symphonies, *Der Freischütz*, *Oberon*, and *A Mid-summer Night's Dream*. But I can still remember very well what a profound impression my father's inspired rendering of the F major passage in the adagio of the 'Ninth' made on the Munich public. He was also a good violinist, and when his weakened lung prevented him from playing the horn he played the viola in the Munich solo string quartet for many years. But the serious asthmatic complaint which remained with him did not prevent him from retaining his position, to his 69th year, as the first horn-player in the Munich Court orchestra, in which capacity he played the whole of *Siegfried* (but without the solo) as late as 1889.

The Baron Perfall mentioned above, who had at one time courted Richard Wagner and Bülow like a humble petitioner, until, on leaving Munich, they recommended him to the King as Intendant of the theatre because they thought they would leave behind in him a faithful supporter, turned out to be an opponent of Wagner as soon as Wagner had left Munich. He succeeded also in removing Bülow. In short, he was a disgusting cad. He treated me in the same way—he commissioned me to rehearse Wagner's *Feen* only to inform me, just before the dress rehearsal, that Court conductor Franz Fischer—who was, by the way, one of the most untalented musicians I have ever met and a real criminal at the rostrum—would now take over the opera since, he, Perfall, could not possibly allow the 'third' conductor to handle such an important new work. Thereupon I handed in my resignation. On the day when I left the Munich Court Theatre, there was a notice on the board announcing the retirement of my father, who had been the most prominent member of the Court Theatre orchestra for forty-five years. Herr von Perfall had not even informed him of his retirement beforehand. In short, he was one of the particular ornaments of Munich, during this not exactly honourable period in the history of my native town.

My father's character had been embittered by a hard youth. He had been orphaned at an early age and went to Nabburg to live with my uncle Walter, who was a warder there and must have been a hard and stern man. My father had to do night-watch duties for him, and during this time he studied a little Latin. At home he was extremely temperamental, quick-tempered, and tyrannical, and my delicate mother required all her meekness and goodness to allow the relationship between my parents, sustained as it always was by genuine love and high esteem, to continue in undisturbed harmony. To what extent the very sensitive nerves of my mother suffered through all this, I cannot today decide. My mother always had to be so careful of her nerves that, although she had an artistic temperament, she was unable to read much and frequently had to pay for visits to the theatre and concerts with sleepless nights. She never uttered a cross word and she was happiest when she was allowed to spend the summer afternoons alone and quietly, busy with her embroidery, in the beautiful garden of my uncle Pschorr's villa, where we children also used to go after school to spend the summer evenings out of doors or playing skittles.

Under my father's strict tutelage I heard nothing but classical music until I was sixteen, and I owe it to this discipline that my love and adoration for the classical masters of music has remained untainted to this day. When I became gradually acquainted with Richard Wagner's works I only remember that the change in *Tannhäuser* from the Venusberg to the Wartburgtal made the greatest impression on me, but that I was quite incapable of appreciating the first performances of *Tristan* and *Siegfried* although I was at that time a fairly well-trained musician, having attended for three years a course in counterpoint given by my excellent and kindly teacher Wilhelm Mayer. I suppose this means that my sense of the dramatic reacted earlier than my musical sense. The prejudices inculcated by upbringing may have influenced me strongly in this. At any rate it was not until, against my father's orders, I studied the score of *Tristan*, that I entered into this magic work, and later into the *Ring des Nibelungen* and I can well remember how, at the age of seventeen, I positively wolfed the score of *Tristan* as if in a trance, and how intoxicated I was with enthusiasm, which was only cooled when I attempted once again to find in the live performance a heightening of the impressions which I had gained through eye and spiritual ear in reading the score. New disappointments and new doubts, new recourse to the score—until I realised at last that it was the discrepancy between a mediocre performance and the intentions of the great master, which I had correctly divined from the score, which prevented the work from sounding in the performance as I had already heard it with the ear of the mind. Having realised this I became (in spite of my old uncle's warnings of the 'swindler of Bayreuth') a 'fully-fledged Wagnerian', and a performance, tolerably in accordance with my wishes, of *Lohengrin* (in which the miracles of orchestration never fail to delight me) or of *Tristan*, or a performance of the *Ring* 'improvised' with the Vienna Philharmonic, remain to this day my greatest joy. Like Anteus after touching the soil, I re-emerge into life with new strength from immersion in the Wagnerian orchestra.

RECOLLECTIONS OF MY YOUTH AND YEARS OF APPRENTICESHIP

MY mother tells of my earliest childhood that I used to react with a smile to the sound of the horn and with loud crying to the sound of a violin. At the age of four and a half I was given my first piano lessons by my father's friend Tombo. My 'cousin' Benno Walter taught me to play the violin and later Niest taught me to play the piano. I was always a bad pupil, because I did not enjoy practising, necessary though it was, whereas I enjoyed playing by sight in order to get to know as many new things as possible. In later years I could also play scores well *Tristan* and Liszt's *Faust Symphony* (which I played for the benefit of good old Alexander Ritter) were my show-pieces. This is the reason why I never managed to become technically efficient (especially as far as my left hand is concerned). My friend Thuille, the 'Pedagogue', used to say in jest: I can tell Richard's fingering from listening in the next room. On the other hand, I was a good accompanist of Lieder—in the free manner, never entirely faithful to the music—because my touch was supposed to be good. I also became a respectable chamber musician. My untrained fingers were, however, defeated by the difficulties of Chopin and Liszt. When Bülow asked me to play a Mozart pianoforte concerto (C minor) with the Meiningen orchestra I had to practise this not really difficult piece—whose simple scales were nevertheless very tricky for me and my left hand—for six months and even then did not master it completely. Moreover I was scared of Bülow who was conducting.

My first attempts at composition (at the age of six) consisted of a Christmas carol, for which I 'painted' the notes myself, but my mother wrote the words below the notes since I could not then write small enough, and the so-called *Schneiderpolka*. These were followed by piano sonatas, Lieder, pieces for horn and clarinet, and later by pieces for chorus and orchestra when I had learned a little orchestration from Mayer. The D minor symphony played in 1881 in the Odeon by Levi was followed by a C minor overture (influenced by *Coriolan*) which was not bad, and then, starting with the E flat major Festival March, I began to get into print.

Eugen Spitzweg, who did much to promote and print my works, although he kept complaining that they did not sell, and was therefore not inclined to be liberal with fees, entered my life when the A major quartet which had first been played by Benno Walter, was turned down by Breitkopf and Härtel. My father contributed one thousand marks to the printing costs of the F minor symphony, but this sum was soon paid back to him.

My first concert tour took me to Vienna, where Benno Walter played my first violin concerto (written into an exercise book in the sixth form at school) while I conducted, and where I received my first and only compliment from Hanslick. When I gave a Lieder recital there twenty years later with my dear wife, he called her my 'better half'. She certainly did sing my Lieder with unrivalled expression and poetic fervour. Nobody even remotely approached her in the singing of *Morgen*, *Traum durch die Dämmerung* or *Jung Hexenlied*. During the winter of 1883 my father treated me to a visit to Berlin. On the way back I called on old Reinecke with a recommendation from Levi, but he refused, with a polite Saxonian smile, to accept even my C minor overture. Radecke was to conduct it in Berlin in the same concert hall in which I was to conduct my rehearsals for 37 years from 1898 onwards. In Berlin I frequented the opera with a free ticket Hülsen had granted me, heard there the old singer Niemann whose voice was no longer at its best in *Tristan*, was made welcome by Klindworth and was on familiar terms with the sculptor Reinhold Begas, whose charming wife I have to thank for many pleasant conversational evenings, and with the painters Carl Becker and Anton von Werner, at whose homes I played string quartets and even made the acquaintance of old Menzel. I was also invited to the house of the poet Spielhagen, who had three particularly charming daughters. Thanks to the hospitality of the Berliners I had a pleasant time. It was at this time that I wrote the F minor symphony.

In 1886 my father made me a present of a first trip to Italy: Verona, Bologna, Rome, Naples, Florence. The result was the *Aus Italien* Suite—During a later Italian jorney to Venice [1888] I invented the first themes of *Don Juan* in the courtyard of the monastery of S. Antonio in Padua.

On the 1st of October [1885] I arrived as conductor in Meiningen and, when Bülow had handed in his resignation owing to the quarrel with Brahms, I was in sole command of the Court orchestra from November to April 1st [1886]. My duty consisted in conducting an orchestral rehearsal every morning at ten o'clock ,when I made the orchestra play to me the whole of their concert repertory. The orchestra gave four concerts in all. The ladies' choral society was also one of my charges. I gave piano lessons to Princess Marie. In the October of that year I met Brahms, who had come for the first performance of his E minor symphony, which had been rehearsed by Bülow. The following extraordinary incident happened during one of the rehearsals. Bülow was not quite sure whether a certain, inaccurately marked, passage should be played *crescendo* and *accelerando* or *diminuendo* and *calando* and asked for Brahms' opinion, after he had played both versions to him. Bülow: 'How do you want it?' Brahms: 'Well, it could be played either way, turn and turn about.' General consternation—Bülow pulled a face. This is what is called 'music as expression'!

In October Bülow was away for three days and I was alone with Brahms every day in the 'Sächsische Hof'. He was quite pleasant and very well read without exhibiting particular signs of genius.

The results of the enthusiasm I then felt for Brahms (under Bülow's suggestive influence) were *Wanderer's Sturmlied* and *Burleske*, which Bülow indignantly criticised as not being pianistic, demanding an unnatural span (his hands were so small that he could only just reach an octave).

Bülow tells this anecdote: When, during a rehearsal of the Ninth symphony, he wanted to get rid of the members of the court who were present, he made the double bassoon rehearse the low passage in the 6/8 of the finale until the 'court' had disappeared.

In February, I had invited Bülow to play and conduct again at a concert for the widows and orphans. Programme: *Eroica*, D minor concerto by Rubinstein, and *Nirwana* by Bülow, a beautiful and neglected piece (originally the overture for a suicide play by Carl Ritter) which I had specially rehearsed for him. The dress rehearsal was sold out, but the Duke, who considered Bülow's departure an insult, did not attend. Only Princess Marie was sitting in a proscenium box in the second gallery. Bülow (annoyed): 'The Duke isn't here. It is really unnecessary for us to rehearse.' I: 'But the Princess is here and the audience will love it'. Bülow then crossed the platform towards the Princess's box and announced: 'Your Highness, His Highness the Duke is not present and it is therefore really superfluous for us to rehearse —but if Your Highness has any special wish . . .' Whereupon Marie said a little tactlessly: 'I would like to hear the *Eroica*'. And Bülow snapped: 'In that case we'll play the pianoforte concerto by Rubinstein.'

I spent many happy hours at Bülow's home. On one occasion he played to me Johann Strauss waltzes. On another I accompanied him to a concert of chamber music in Weimar. Irritated as he always was in Weimar, he snapped at Conductor Mueller-

Hartung who met him at the station: 'this damned hole Weimar, where no Brahms symphony is ever played'—'You're wrong, Herr Doktor, I have conducted all the Brahms symphonies here': Bülow, sarcastically: 'But how'.

My stay in Meiningen was all the more important to me because the theatre did not go on tour that winter and I had an opportunity of admiring the wonderful performances of the classics, arranged by Duke George, which excelled particularly in the careful handling of crowd scenes and in faithful productions. The first and coronation acts of the *Jungfrau von Orleans*, the entry of the cuirassiers in *Wallenstein* and *Julius Caesar* will always stay in my memory. An example of the Duke's working methods: On New Year's Eve the rehearsal went on until nine o'clock, ten o'clock, and at last the clock struck midnight; the Duke rose, and everyone heaved a sigh of relief. Thereupon the Duke: 'I wish you all a happy New Year. The rehearsal will now continue'. Those were the days when the eight hour working day was unheard of.

As far as I was concerned the greatest event of the winter in Meiningen was my acquaintance with Alexander Ritter, who was one of the first violins in the orchestra. He was the son of that fine woman Julie Ritter, who had supported Richard Wagner for years, and the husband of Franziska, née Wagner, the master's niece. He invited me to his house, where I found the spiritual stimulus which was the decisive factor in my further development.

As a result of my upbringing, I still had some prejudices against Wagner's and especially against Liszt's work, and I scarcely knew Richard Wagner's writings at all. Ritter, with patient explanations, introduced me to them and to Schopenhauer; he made me familiar with them and proved to me that the road led from the 'musical express ionist' Beethoven ('music as expression' in Friedrich von Hausegger's phrase as against Hanslick's 'Of

Beauty in Music') via Liszt who, with Wagner, had realised correctly that Beethoven had expanded the sonata form to its utmost limits—in Anton Bruckner, the 'stammering cyclops', it actually explodes these limits, particularly in the finales—and that in Beethoven's epigones and especially in Brahms, sonata form had become an empty shell, in which Hanslick's high-sounding phrases, the invention of which required little imagination and personal aptitude for form, could easily be accommodated. Hence so much that is insignificant in Brahms and Bruckner, especially in the transition passages.

New ideas must search for new forms—this basic principle of Liszt's symphonic works in which the poetic idea was really the formative element, became from that day on the guiding principle for my own symphonic work. The first hesitant attempt was made in the suite *Aus Italien*, by transposition of the movements and, as in the third movement (*Sorrento*), of the constituent parts of movements. *Macbeth* had to be altered first, on the advice of Bülow, in accordance with the correct stylistic principles of the genuine composer of programme music. In reality, of course, there is no programme music so-called. This is merely a term of abuse used by all those who are incapable of being original. In the same way the word trash is preferred by those who, like the fox, coveting the grapes, are jealous of the 'effect' made by a *Tannhäuser* or *Oberon* overture or by Schiller's *Räuber*. Bülow was shocked even at the dissonances of *Macbeth*, but remarked very properly that the first final triumphal march in D major of Macduff was nonsense. It was all very well for an Egmont overture to conclude with a triumphal march of Egmont, but a symphonic poem *Macbeth* could never finish with the triumph of Macduff. A poetic programme may well suggest new forms, but whenever music is not developed logically from within, it becomes 'literary music'. When in 1894 I myself conducted *Macbeth* at a concert in Berlin, Bülow patted me on the back after the performance and said: 'It's quite a good piece after all'. I am indebted to Ritter for suggesting the *Guntram* text although it became the cause of our estrangement. When during my stay in Egypt I became familiar with the works of Nietzsche, whose polemic against Christianity was particularly to my liking, the antipathy which I had always felt against a religion which relieves the faithful of responsibility for their actions (by means of confession) was confirmed and strengthened. Ritter could never quite forgive me for the renunciation of society (Third act, Guntram-Friedhold scene) when Guntram judges himself and abrogates the right of the community to punish him.

In October 1886 I began my areer as third Musical Director in Munich. My first operas were *Johann von Paris*, and, curiously enough, *Cosi fan tutte* even then in which Heinrich Vogl gave me his good advice about not conducting with 'too long an arm'. I have observed this ever since. Vogl like to be sparing with his voice, loved fluid tempi and rightly felt that the long lever attached to the conductor's shoulder joint handicapped him. I was not a particularly good third conductor. Although I was handy as a substitute—I tackled an opera by Rheinberger even at this early stage—I was frequently handicapped in the smooth execution of my duties as an operative conductor by my lack of 'routine' in which many colleagues of lesser talents were for a long time to be my masters, and by my stubborn insistence on 'my own tempi'. There were, therefore, quite a few upsets, and the usual disagreements between singers and orchestra, especially since the operas I had to conduct at that time did not interest me sufficiently to make me rehearse them carefully, and would really have required far more careful study before the rehearsals —a task which in works like *Nachtlager* and *Martha* bored me far too much.

From Munich I once tried to get a transfer to Hanover. Bülow refused to give me a recommendation with the words: 'Why exchange the Hanoverians of the South for the Bavarians of the North?' In 1889 Bülow's friend Hans von Bronsart appointed me second conductor in Weimar with Eduard Lassen.

The time which followed was wonderful. In Weimar I won my beloved Pauline, who had followed me as a pupil and was appointed after one year as a singer of youthful dramatic roles. She was an excellent Pamina, Elvira, Elsa, Elisabeth and Evchen and even had the pluck to sing Fidelio and Isolde (too early, of course, but somehow because of her youth and great acting a particularly charming performance). By creating the roles of Hänsel and Freihild she made the hearts of the authors (Humperdinck and myself) beat faster. It was at this time that Cosima Wagner, who was to be my friend for many years, began to take an interest in us, and when she came to Weimar for a performance of *Lohengrin* which I conducted, she chose Pauline for the roles of flower girl and shepherd. This led to the role of Elisabeth at the 1891 festival, after Cosima Wagner had made Pauline's closer acquaintance during a concert in Bayreuth when she sang Liszt's Elizabeth. I was chosen to conduct *Tannhäuser*, but was unable to do so owing to a serious attack of pneumonia which I contracted in the spring of 1891 in the park at Tiefurt. When, a year later, I had another slight attack of pleurisy, my uncle Georg Pschorr generously sent me to Egypt with 5000 Marks so that I could convalesce fully. On the way out I spent the month of November in Corfu, Olympia and Athens, a stay which was to determine my whole attitude towards Greek civilisation and especially towards the art of the 4th and 5th centuries B.C. In Luxor I scored the first act of *Guntram* which was first performed in Weimar in May 1894. The theatre bill lists the best artists with whom I have ever worked; especially the good tenor Heinrich Zeller. The other singers were the dramatic soprano Naumann-Gungel, the heroic tenor Denis Stavenhagen, and the soubrette Kayser. As far as I was concerned, my first great experience was

Lohengrin, which was followed by *Tannhäuser*, *The Flying Dutchman* and finally *Tristan*. Apart from the symphony concerts (Ninth Symphony!) there were Mozart's *Don Giovanni*, *Magic Flute*, *Fidelio*, a new presentation by Cosima Wagner of *Rienzi*, *Das eisene Pferd* by Humperdinck-Auber, *Freischütz*, *Euryanthe*, *Iphigenie in Aulis*—which prompted me to work on *Iphigenie auf Tauris* as well. Several new works by R. Metzdorff, Mottl and finally Alexander Ritter's *Fauler Hans* and *Wem die Krone?*

As far as compositions are concerned, the yield of the Weimar period apart from *Guntram* and a few good songs (*Caecilie*, *Heimliche Aufforderung*) was not very good, since the theatre and cards, as well as my fiancée, claimed almost all my attention. On the whole, people were very nice to me (Bronsart, Lassen, the Court); but I recklessly squandered some of the good-will they bore me, by my youthful energy and love of exaggeration, so that people were not sorry to see Pauline and me leave, when in 1894 I received from Possart a second call to Munich as first conductor (as substitute for Herman Levi who was ailing).

My second period in Munich was spoiled mainly by the bad feeling between Possart (Court Theatre), who was well-disposed towards me, and Perfall (Hofmusikintendant), who became more hostile towards me with every new work (*Till Eulenspiegel*, *Zarathustra*). Indignantly he broadcast my joke in *Jugend*—a song which ended half a note higher than it began. I conducted the Akademie-Konzerte for two years but because the programmes were too modern—the two sea pieces by Schillings in particular aroused the dismay of conservative philistines. I was replaced by Erdmannsdorfer. On top of this disagreement there came the failure of *Guntram*, against which the orchestra (led by my good cousin Benno Walter) had protested even during the rehearsals, calling it a 'scourge of God'. Vogl and Ternina had returned their parts, as being 'too high'. Mikorey had failed to master his part before the performance, and only Pauline's performance as 'Freihild' was excellent. When Mikorey refused to give a repeat performance and asked for a higher pension the opera fell into oblivion. But at least I conducted *Tristan* and *Meistersinger* in Munich, and perfected my technique; and although many people, especially the Wagnerians in the *Münchner Neuesten Nachrichten* and the old fogies in the *Sammler*, found fault with me, I was given opportunities of travelling extensively abroad (Paris, Barcelona, etc.), and spent precious hours in the company of Friedrich Rösch and Alexander Ritter. From six to seven o'clock in the evening we could be found in Leidenfrost's Weinstube, and I frequently spent evenings in Ritter's house.

When in 1898 I was offered a position for life in Munich, Perfall attempted at the last moment to reduce the salary which had been agreed upon, so since Weingartner was retiring, I took the opportunity of going to Berlin, was immediately appointed with Muck by Hochberg and Pierson, at a salary of 20,000 Mark, and had no reason ever to regret this connection with Berlin; on the whole, my stay in Berlin was pure joy, and I found there much appreciation and hospitality. Fifteen years' experience of symphony concerts with the Royal Orchestra provided hours of wonderful artistic enjoyment and endeavour. These connections with the Berlin State Opera have survived all temporary separation (Vienna). After *Feuersnot* had been given a successful first performance in Dresden under the courageous and excellent Schuch, it was performed in the following autumn with Berger and Destinn under my baton in Berlin, but was prohibited after the seventh performance by the Kaiser because the Empress had taken offence, whereupon Hochberg handed in his resignation, for which I would like to thank him here once again. For the sake of decency Georg von Hülsen put on the opera a few more times after this, with the Kaiser's permission, but in accordance with the wishes of the all-highest then allowed it to die a natural death. By his loving attention to my later operas he more than compensated for this first mishap.

I made numerous concert tours from Munich; while I was at Weimar I had begun to conduct a large number of works by Liszt in the "Leipzig Liszt Verein" almost every year, that great master who is misunderstood as well as unappreciated to this day (especially by professional musicians and the critics under their influence). I first conducted *Don Juan* in Weimar, and *Death and Transfiguration* at the music festival at Eisenach in 1890. In the same concert Eugen d'Albert conducted a magnificent first performance of my *Burlesk*. The first performance of *Aus Italien* aroused strong opposition in Munich. The pianist Giebel made the following joke: 'It is easy to tell from the finale that Strauss visited Naples immediately after the cholera'. It was also at this time that Berlioz' *Fee Mab* was hissed in the Odeon because of his liberal use of the kitchen, as my father called the percussion instruments. What would people say today! Bülow himself was to conduct *Aus Italien* in Italy, and I followed with *Don Juan*, *Death and Transfiguration*, and *Macbeth*. When this wonderful man and artist died all too soon in 1894 I took over his philharmonic concerts (in Berlin). Precocious though I was, I was slow in becoming a conductor, and was unable to hold my own after this great man. In 1895, H. Wolff put the magnificent Nikisch in charge of the concerts and I had to be content with my 7000 marks in Munich. As proof that I have never failed to promote selflessly the interests of any talented colleague, I would like to point out here that I recommended Reger to Spitzweg (who immediately printed the first 25 works of this prolific master of the organ), and that I either conducted the first performances of Mahler's first four symphonies myself—the first in Weimar, the second in Berlin, where Lessmann abused me as follows: 'The altar consecrated by Bülow has now been defiled by pygmies'— or put them on my programmes, as when Mahler himself conducted the fourth in Berlin. The second and third symphonies I put on the programmes of the music festivals in Basle and Essen. Further I would mention the first performance of Humperdinck's *Hänsel und Gretel* in Weimar, and of Schillings' *Ingwelde* in Munich. In Berlin, apart from the opera, I conducted the mediocre "Tonkünstler Orchestra" for three years in concerts of exclusively new works, a difficult task. The following was the schedule of a typical working day: 11 to 2 o'clock, orchestral rehearsal for *Don Juan*, 3 to 6 o'clock third Bruckner symphony, and *Tristan* at night.

REMINISCENCES OF THE FIRST PERFORMANCE
OF MY OPERAS
From *Guntram* to *Intermezzo*

BERLIOZ writes in his article on *Fidelio*: 'Grétry has accused Mozart of putting the pedestal on the stage and the statue in the orchestra—an accusation previously levelled at Gluck and later at Weber, Spontini and Beethoven, which will always be levelled at all composers, in spite of all careful restraint, as soon as they refrain from writing platitudes for the singers and attempt instead to give the orchestra an interesting part to play, etc.' This seems to me to be a good motto for my experiences with my operas and their development.

I should like to start with

Guntram.

The subject was suggested by Alexander Ritter. I am indebted to him for the discovery of my dramatic vocation. Without his encouragement and co-operation it would hardly have occurred to me to write an opera, over-awed as I was by Richard Wagner's gigantic work, since there were no suitable librettists, or rather since, like Eberhard König (who later wrote for Hans Sommer) they did not stimulate me. I was at that time under the influence of Ritter, who had written for his own use two very nice libretti (*Der faule Hans* and *Wem die Krone*), and was thus firmly convinced that an operatic composer should write his own libretti—but unfortunately I lacked 'poetic' talent. A few drafts—amongst others *Eulenspiegel* and *Die Schildbürger*—did not get beyond the initial stages.

Ritter, who sympathised and encouraged me, unfortunately set his face against *Guntram* when I formed the third act in accordance with my own ideas, and instead of letting Guntram return to face the judgment of the 'Community' as Ritter wanted me to do, made him be his own judge, which was against Ritter's philosophy. The score of the first act was completed in Luxor in 1893 and the opera was accepted for the spring of 1894 by Weimar, where the orchestra at that time consisted of six first and five second violins, four violas, three 'celli and three double basses! The third horns, which were recruited from the military band when needed, accorded ill with those of the Court orchestra, probably even in Liszt's days (cf. the three flutes in the third act of *Tannhäuser*). But *Guntram* with a score which in no way suited conditions there and is moreover a proof of my incredible naïveté at that time, was rehearsed; my poor and courageous pupil, Heinrich Zeller, suffered torments with the insanely taxing vocal part—people calculated at the time that his rôle contained so-and-so many bars more than *Tristan*—became hoarser with each rehearsal and only finished the first performance with difficulty. My fiancée, as she then was, mastered her part completely and gave a performance which was excellently sung as well as acted. After the second act she was enthusiastically applauded in Weimar, as also later in the disastrous Munich performance.

In the course of one of the last rehearsals, when I had to interrupt Zeller time and again, we at last came to Pauline's scene in the third act which she obviously knew. In spite of this she did not feel sure of herself and apparently envied Zeller because he had been giving so many chances of 'repeating'. Suddenly she stopped singing, and asked me: 'Why don't you interrupt me?' I replied: 'Because you know your part.' With the words 'I want to be interrupted', she threw the piano score which she happened to be holding in her hand at my head but, to the delight of the orchestra, it landed on the desk of the second violinist Gutheil (later to become the husband of the famous Madame Gutheil-Schoder, who made her début under me in that same year as Pamina and Hänsel).

Guntram scored a *succès d'éstime*, but after a few futile attempts to revive it in Frankfort and Prague by making extensive cuts it vanished completely from the stage, and with it disappeared for the next six years my courage in writing for the theatre.

A single unfortunate performance was given in Munich. The leading singers there, Madame Ternina and Heinrich Vogl, had refused to sing their parts, the orchestra, too, under the leadership of my own cousin and violin teacher, the Konzertmeister Benno Walter, had gone on strike, and a deputation had been sent to the Generalintendant, Perfall, to ask him to spare the orchestra this 'scourge of God'. The tenor Mikorey, whose memory had failed in places even during the first performance, declared afterwards that he would only sing in further performances if his pension was increased. Thus there was no second performance, until, on my seventieth birthday, Berlin radio broadcast a concert performance with extensive cuts under Rosbaud, which showed that this work—in spite of the many first performances there had been since 1894—contained so much beautiful music that *Guntram* well deserved a revival, if only because of its historic interest as the first work of a dramatist who was later to become successful. Thereupon I published a new edition with cuts, which had a magnificent resurrection in Weimar in 1940 under Sixt; the second half of the second act and the whole of the third act made a strong impression and even I had to confess that, compared with all the operas which had been written apart from mine in the past forty years, the work was still 'viable'. In the meantime, *Guntram* has been accepted by the Berlin State Opera, where it is sure to make its full impression for the first time with the large orchestra there. * In Weimar

---

*The first performance in Berlin took place under Robert Heger on the 13th June, 1942.

Freihild was excellent and Guntram was praiseworthy, if only because of his stamina, although intellectually he was not quite equal to his task. But even there the misfortune which had dogged the work from the beginning held: the singer was unable to go on singing the part because of a protracted illness.

Feuersnot

After the failure of *Guntram* I had lost the courage to write for the stage. It was then that I came across the Flemish legend, *The Quenched Fires of Audenarde*, which gave me the idea of writing, with personal motives, a little intermezzo against the theatre. To wreak some vengeance on my dear native town where I, little Richard the third (there is no 'second', Hans von Bülow once said) had just like the great Richard the first thirty years before, had such unpleasant experiences. The good Ernst von Schuch had accepted *Feuersnot* and, in spite of some moral objections, it was very successfully performed in Dresden with the wonderful Karl Scheidemantel and Annie Krull. Its subsequent fate—especially in Berlin, where it had to be removed from the repertoire after the seventh performance at the instance of the Empress, whereupon the honest Generalintendant Count Hochberg handed in his resignation—is well known. Unfortunately, *Feuersnot* is comparatively difficult, requiring a superior baritone who can easily reach the heights, a good many solo singers capable of good characterisation, and containing difficult children's choruses, which have always been a handicap in repertoire performances. And then Kunrad's great address still fails to be appreciated by audiences used to *Il Trovatore* and *Martha*. I wonder whether this will ever change. Ernst von Wolzogen, who wrote this pretty, truly popular libretto for me, later arranged a short story by Cervantes which I had already planned as a one-act opera. I have mislaid the libretto I know not where.

Salome

Once, in Berlin, I went to Max Reinhardt's 'Little Theatre' in order to see Gertrud Eysoldt in Oscar Wilde's *Salome*. After the performance I met Heinrich Grünfeld, who said to me: 'My dear Strauss, surely you could make an opera of this'! I replied: 'I am already busy composing it'. The Viennese poet Anton Lindtner had sent me this exquisite play and had offered to turn it into a libretto for me. When I agreed, he sent me a few cleverly versified opening scenes, but I could not make up my mind to start composing until one day it occurred to me to set to music *Wie schön ist die Prinzessin Salome heute Nacht* straight away. From then on it was not difficult to purge the piece of purple passages to such an extent that it became quite a good libretto. Now, of course, that the dance and especially the whole finale scene is steeped in music it is easy to say that the play was 'simply calling for music'. Yes, indeed, but that had to be discovered.

I had long been criticising the fact that operas based on oriental and Jewish subjects lacked true oriental colour and scorching sun. The needs of the moment inspired me with truly exotic harmonies, which sparkled like taffeta particularly in the strange cadences. The wish to characterise the *dramatis personae* as clearly as possible led me to bitonality, since the purely rhythmic characterisation Mozart uses so ingeniously did not appear to me sufficient to express the antithesis between Herod and the Nazarene. This may well stand as a unique experiment with a peculiar subject, but it cannot be recommended to imitators. As soon as Schuch had had the courage to undertake to produce *Salome*, the difficulties began: during the first reading rehearsal at the piano, the assembled soloists returned their parts to the conductor with the single exception of Mr. Burian, a Czech, who, when asked for his opinion last of all, replied: 'I know it off by heart already'. Good for him. After this the others could not help feeling a little ashamed and rehearsals actually started. During the casting rehearsals Frau Wittich, entrusted the part of the sixteen-year-old Princess with the voice of Isolde (one just does not write a thing like that, Herr Strauss: either one or the other), because of the strenuous nature of the part and the strength of the orchestra, went on strike with the indignant protest to be expected from the wife of a Saxon Burgomaster: 'I won't do it, I'm a decent woman', thereby reducing the producer Wirk, who was all for 'perversity and outrage' to desperation. And yet Frau Wittich, although of course her figure was unsuitable for the part, was quite right (if in a different sense): the capers cut in later performances by exotic variety stars indulging in snakelike movements and waving Jochanaan's head about in the air went beyond all bounds of decency and good taste. Anyone who has been in the east and has observed the decorum with which women there behave, will appreciate that Salome, being a chaste virgin and an oriental princess, must be played with the simplest and most restrained of gestures, unless her defeat by the miracle of a great world is to excite only disgust and terror instead of sympathy. (In connection with this I should like to point out that the high B flat of the double bass during the killing of the Baptist does not represent cries of pain uttered by the victim, but sighs of anguish from the heart of an impatiently expectant Salome. The ominous passage proved so shocking during the dress rehearsal that Graf Seebach, for fear of causing merriment, pursuaded me to tone the double bass down by a sustained B flat on the English horns.) Generally speaking, the acting of the singers should, of course, in contrast with the excessive turmoil of the music, be limited to the utmost simplicity; Herod in particular must remember, amidst the comings and goings of the hysterical crowd, that he should endeavour, oriental parvenu though he is, to preserve his dignity and composure before his Roman guests, in imitation of the greater Caesar in Rome, notwithstanding all momentary erotic misdemeanour. Turmoil on and in front of the stage simultaneously—that would be too much. The orchestra alone is quite adequate—when I played to my father from the score of Salome on the piano a few months before his death, he said in desperation: 'Oh God, what nervous music. It is exactly as if one had one's trousers full of Maybugs'. He was not entirely wrong. Cosima Wagner who insisted against my advice that I should play something from the opera to her in Berlin, remarked after the final scene: 'This is absolute madness. You are for the exotic, Siegfried for the popular!' Clang!

The first performance in Dresden was, as usual, a success, but the critics gathered together in the Bellevue Hotel after the performance, shook their heads and agreed that the piece would perhaps be performed by a few of the largest theatres but would soon disappear. Three weeks later it had, I think, been accepted by ten theatres and had been a sensational success in Breslau with an orchestra of 70 players. Thereupon there was a hulla-baloo in the papers, the churches objected—the first performance in the Vienna State Opera took place in October 1918, after an embarrassing exchange of letters with Archbishop Piffl—and so did the Puritans in New York, where the opera had to be taken off the repertoire at the instigation of a certain Mr. Morgan. The German Kaiser only permitted the performance of the opera after Hülsen had had the bright idea of signifying the advent of the Magi at the end by the appearance of the morning star! William the Second once said to his Intendant: 'I am sorry Strauss composed this *Salome*. I really like the fellow, but this will do him a lot of damage'. The damage enabled me to build the villa in Garmisch. In connection with this I remember with gratitude the Berlin publisher, Adolph Fürstner, who had the courage to print the opera, for which other colleagues (e.g. Hugo Bock) did not at first envy him in the least. But by so doing this wise and kind Jew had also secured for himself *Der Rosenkavalier*. All honour to his memory!

An Italian impresario who could not pay Fürstner's fees and was unable to get hold of a printed score had commissioned a small Kapellmeister to make a new one from the piano score(!) and intended, without our authority, to perform the opera in this form in Holland, which, I understand, was outside the Berne Convention at that time. When Fürstner heard of this he negotiated with the impresario and eventually persuaded him to hand over his new score to us, and to perform the opera in accordance with my score, provided I conducted the performance in Amsterdam myself. I considered it my duty 'to save my opera' ('What an ass I was' to quote from *Ariadne*) and accepted the offer. But what I was to find in Amsterdam beggars all description. I had at my disposal for *one* dress rehearsal a miserable Italian troupe hardly capable of managing more than a sixth-grade performance of *Il Trovatore* and which did not know its parts, and a beer garden orchestra, which would have required at least twenty rehearsals to be made more or less presentable. It was dreadful and yet I could not resign without risking an enormous indemnity. In the circumstances, it had to be carried through to the bitter end. I concluded the evening full of shame and annoyance and, believe it or not, my old friend Justizrat Fritz Sieger, who had been my patron in the Frankfurt Museum ever since the F Minor Symphony, and who had by chance attended the performance, told me afterwards that it had been quite a good performance and he had liked it very well indeed. Can it be that the hypnotism of my baton was such that even a connoisseur overlooked the shortcomings of the performance, or is it simply impossible to kill the opera? I think the latter must have been the case since, when I saw the piece in Innsbruck two years ago with redoubled woodwind (an orchestra of 56 players) and admittedly good soloists—that excellent Swede, Madam Sönderquist—I had to admit that it made its effect in spite of these limitations. The moral of all this is: How many lines of the score could I not have saved myself from the beginning, had I written a score like the clever little Italian conductor whose orchestration was designed for seasons in Ferrara and Piacenza. But these *L'art pour l'art* artists who will never compose 'mysteries of the national soul' (*Münchner Neueste Nachrichten*, 9th February, 1942) will heed no advice. The secret of the forty-line page of a score is after all greater than that of a 'romantic' purse.

Elektra

When I first saw Hofmannsthal's inspired play in the *Deutsche Theater* with Gertrud Eysoldt, I immediately recognised, of course, what a magnificent operatic libretto it might be (after the alteration I made in the Orestes scene it has actually become one) and, just as previously with *Salome*, I appreciated the tremendous increase in musical tension to the very end: In *Elektra*, after the recognition scene, which could only be completely realised in music, the release in dance—in *Salome*, after the dance (the heart of the plot), the dreadful apotheosis of the end. Both operas offered wonderful musical points of attack:

Salome: the contrasts; the court of Herod, Jochanaan, the Jews, the Nazarenes.

Elektra: the possessed goddess of vengeance contrasted with the radiant character of her mortal sister.

Salome: the three seduction songs of Salome, Herod's three persuasive speeches,

Salome's ostinato: *Ich will den Kopf des Jochanaan* ('I want the head of Jochanaan').

Elektra: the first monologue; the unending climaxes
in the scene between Elektra and Chrysothemis
in the scene between Elektra and Clytaemnestra
(both unfortunately still extensively cut).

But at first I was put off by the idea that both subjects were very similar in psychological content, so that I doubted whether

I should have the power to exhaust this subject also. But the wish to contrast this possessed, exalted Greece of the 6th century with Winckelmann's Roman copies and Goethe's humanism outweighed these doubts, and *Elektra* became even more intense in the unity of structure and in the force of its climaxes. I am almost tempted to say that it is to *Salome* what the more flawless, and stylistically more uniform *Lohengrin* is to the inspired first venture of *Tannhäuser*. Both operas are unique in my life's works, in them I penetrated to the uttermost limits of harmony, psychological polyphony (Clytemnaestra's dream) and of the receptivity of modern ears.

Since there are many stories told about me which are quite untrue, I would like to add here a few authentic but harmless *Elektra* anecdotes.

During one of the first orchestral rehearsals Schuch, who was very sensitive to draughts, noticed in the third balcony of the empty theatre a door which had been left open by a charwoman. Full of annoyance, he shouted: 'What are you looking for?', I replied from the front stalls: 'A triad'.

A middle-aged excellent clarinetist (a Czech) of the Vienna orchestra stayed behind at his place after a rehearsal to clean his instrument. When at last he put it back in its case he mumbled with resignation: 'If only a Czech had written this'.

A solid Swiss was asked after a performance in Basle how he had liked the opera. 'It was wonderful!'—'And the music?'—I heard no music'. I prefer such a listener to a criticising amateur who may not have understood the music at all.

The performance of *Elektra* had again been extremely carefully prepared by the conscientious Schuch. Once again he knew the score as well as if it were the twentieth performance. Schuch was famous for his elegant performances of Italian and French operas and as a discreet accompanist. He had perfected this praiseworthy art to such a pitch that under him even Wagner's scores sounded a little undistinguished. One hardly ever heard a real fortissimo from the brass of this exemplary Dresden orchestra. Since at that time, thirty-five years ago, I was still enamoured of the teutonic *ff*, I was stupid enough to find fault during rehearsals with Schuch's euphonious (but not incisive) brass, which annoyed him. I insisted that hearing my score for the first time I should hear the whole complexity of the score, completely forgetting that such complicated polyphony will only become quite plastic and lucid after years, when the orchestra has it almost by heart. Schuch, being a friend of the poor 'declaiming' singers, had already toned down the orchestra in the first few rehearsals to such an extent that it sounded too colourless for my liking, although the singers at least could be heard. My continued insistence on secondary thematic parts annoyed Schuch so much that he played with such fury during the dress rehearsal that I was forced to make the humble confession: 'The orchestra was really a little too strong today'—'You see', said Schuch triumphantly, and the first performance had perfect balance.

Only Frau Schumann-Heink (the famous Wagner singer) who gave a guest performance as Clytemnæstra was shown to be miscast. I cannot use old 'stars'—I was beginning to realise at that time how fundamentally my vocal style differs even from that of Wagner. My vocal style has the pace of a stage play and frequently comes into conflict with the figuring and polyphony of the orchestra, so that none but the best conductors, who themselves know something of singing, can establish the balance of volume and speed between singer and baton. The struggle between word and music has been the problem of my life right from the beginning, which *Capriccio* solves with a question mark. The first performance was a *succès d'éstime*, but, as usual, I did not learn this until later. Angelo Neumann even wired to Prague: 'Failure'. Many now consider *Elektra* the acme of my work. Others give their vote to *Frau ohne Schatten*. The majority swears by *Rosenkavalier*. One must be content to have achieved so much as a German composer. Of the singers of *Elektra*, I would like to mention the following with special gratitude: Annie Krull (Dresden), Thila Plaichinger (Berlin), Edith Walker (Hamburg), Alice Sanden (Leipzig), Zdenka Fassbender (Munich), Marie Gutheil-Schoder (Vienna), Gertrud Rünger (Vienna), and also Madame Kruzeniska of the Scala, Milan, who was equally perfect as Salome and as Elektra.

Der Rosenkavalier

When I gave Hofmannsthal's libretto to my Berlin Intendant, Graf Hülsen, to read he advised me against it: 'Not', he said, 'a libretto for you'. He regretted that he himself was so busy, otherwise he himself would have written a 'real German libretto' for me. After the hundredth performance in Berlin he came to my room and congratulated me with the words, 'But what a charming libretto it is'. Details of Hülsen's alterations to render the piece palatable to the German Kaiserin can be found in the report of the State Opera for 1934 on the occasion of my 60th birthday.

Der Rosenkavalier is the only one of my operas which Kaiser Wilhelm attended, at the suggestion of the Crown Prince, but he left with the words: 'This is no music for me'.

When, in Dresden, I listened to the first stage rehearsal with orchestra, I realised during the second act that the producer of the old school who was in charge was completely incapable of producing the opera. Alfred Roller's stage designs were excellent and have remained exemplary to this day. All honour to his memory! Remembering a kind offer made by Max Reinhardt I asked Generalintendant Graf Seebach whether I could invite Reinhardt to come and help us. Seebach reluctantly permitted this on the condition that Reinhardt would not set foot on the stage. Reinhardt came without making demands and, Jew and art en-

thusiast that he was, even accepted the above condition, and thus
we all met on the rehearsal stage, Reinhardt as a modest spectator, whilst I in my clumsy way showed the singers as best I could
how to play their parts. After a while Reinhardt could be observed whispering to Frau von der Osten in a corner of the hall
and then again with Miss Siems, Perron, etc.

The next day they came to the rehearsal transformed into full-
fledged actors. Thereupon Seebach graciously permitted Reinhardt to direct operations on the stage instead of watching the
rehearsal from the stalls. The result was a new style in opera and
a perfect performance in which the trio in particular (Siems, von
der Osten, Nast) delighted everybody.

The evening was a little long drawn out, since, in my enthusiasm, I had composed the whole of the somewhat talkative text
without alteration, although even the author had expected me
to make cuts. Cuts were Schuch's speciality; he never, I believe,
conducted an opera without cuts and was particularly proud
when he could leave out a whole act of a modern opera. Immediately after my departure he proceeded to make the most dreadful cuts in *Rosenkavalier*, which were immediately copied by the
thoughtless directors of other theatres; I had to fight for years
against this stupidity. It is not true that a well-composed and
dramatically carefully arranged opera is made shorter by cuts.
For example, a year later Seebach's friend, Baroness Knorring,
came to Berlin and saw 'my' *Rosenkavalier*. Afterwards she told
me the opera had seemed to her shorter than in Dresden. I replied: 'Yes, because there were fewer cuts in it'. The proportions
were better, and light and shade were better distributed.

After I had borne my annoyance at Schuch's ineradicable cuts
for some time, I wrote to him saying that he had forgotten one
important cut; the trio in the third act only impeded the action,
and I suggested the following cuts: D major: 'Ich weiss nix,
garnix' to G major: beginning of the last duet. This offended him

but at last he was cured to some extent of the Dresden disease. Schuch's predecessor once came to Draeseke and said: 'I hear you have completed a new opera'. Draeseke replied: 'Well, the opera itself is finished, only the cuts must still be composed'.

The triumphant career of *Der Rosenkavalier* was tragi-comically interrupted in the Scala, Milan. Serafin had rehearsed the opera faultlessly with an excellent cast: Madam Bori as Octavian, Ludikar as Ochs, very good, but with a slight Bohemian accent, which shocked the Italians who were sensitive enough in this respect, all the more, as they imagined that they had the monopoly of such (somewhat vulgar) buffo parts in their Italian comic operas. Pauline and I sat in the Proscenium box with the Duke Visconti and his wife, with whom Pauline discussed French fashions. After a while the latter said to her: 'I think you and your husband are the only people in the theatre tonight who are not nervous'. Pauline: 'Why should I be nervous? The opera has done quite well in Germany'. The end of the second act was to show how right the Principessa was. The first act went well, with three curtain calls. After a second act there was not a sign of applause, but turmoil broke loose: Hissing, whistling, and shouting, whilst hundreds of pamphlets were scattered from the top balcony where the younger generation (at that time they called themselves 'futurists') were protesting against the 'debasement' in this lighthearted work of the author of *Salome*. When the noise had subsided I went on the stage and asked what had annoyed the people? The reply was: 'the waltz'. I said: 'But why the waltz?' The producer: 'Well, in La Scala the audience only stomach the "Viennese Waltz" in Ballet.' I said with a laugh: 'What will happen in the third act? There'll be a few more waltzes'. They shrugged their shoulders—the third act began: absolute silence during the introductory fugato (*musica seria tedesca*), then the E major waltz was played again behind the scene. When Madam Bori sang: *Che bella musica*, a sarcastic voice called from the gods: '*Eh—bella musica*' and the turmoil started anew and reached its climax with Lerchenau's exit. I kept glancing at the curtain, wondering when it would come down. It did not come down—the audience gradually calmed down until the trio commenced in absolute silence. After that there was wild applause—the evening was saved. Three cheers for the Italians who have preserved an independent judgment, even if they make mistakes occasionally. After the second performance the waltz was always played piano, so as to shock the irredentist snobs less. After four performances the opera disappeared from the repertoire, to be triumphantly revived even in Italy several years later. Apart from this, every first performance in the Scala becomes a struggle between the rival publishers Ricordi and Sonzogno. After the third act of *Rosenkavalier* the fight was continued between the orchestra and the first row of the stalls, at which the conductor shouted: "Asini."

Two important hints to the actors: Just as Clytemnæstra should not be an old hag, but a beautiful proud woman of fifty, whose ruin is purely spiritual and by no means physical, the Marschallin must be a young and beautiful woman of 32 at the most who, in a bad mood, thinks herself 'an old woman' as compared with the seventeen-year-old Octavian, but who is not by any means David's Magdalena, who, by the way, is also frequently presented as too old. Octavian is neither the first nor the last lover of the beautiful Marschallin, nor must the latter play the end of the first act sentimentally as a tragic farewell to life but with Viennese grace and lightness, half-weeping, half smiling. The conductor should not slow down too much, starting with the F major 2/4. The figure which has so far been most misunderstood is that of Ochs. Most basses have presented him as a disgusting vulgar monster with a repellent mask and proletarian manners, and this has rightly shocked civilised audiences (the French and Italians). This is quite wrong: Ochs must be a rustic beau of thirty-five, who is after all a member of the gentry, if somewhat countryfied, and who is capable of behaving properly in the salon of the Marschallin without running the risk of being thrown out by her servants after five minutes. He is at heart a cad, but outwardly still so presentable that Faninal does not refuse him at first sight. Especially Ochs's first scene in the bedroom must be played with utmost delicacy and discretion if it is not to be as disgusting as the love affair of a general's elderly wife with a cadet. In other words: Viennese comedy, not— Berlin farce.

Ariadne auf Naxos

Intended by Hofmannsthal as a grateful offering to Max Reinhardt as the epilogue to a comedy by Molière, *Ariadne*, split into three parts—provided (like a well known mythological snake) with nine heads—was eventually resolved into two new comedies. The first idea was fascinating: beginning in the most sober of comic prose and proceeding via ballet and *commedia dell'arte* to the heights of the purest symphonic music, it failed at last owing to a certain lack of culture on the part of the audience. The play-going public did not get its money's worth, the opera public did not know what to make of Molière. The producer had to put on dramatic and operatic casts simultaneously and instead of two box-office successes he had one doubtful one.

But let us start with the history of the opera: I enjoyed composing the incidental music to the play which, like almost everything I dashed off, as it were, 'with my left hand', became so good that it continued its existence successfully as a small suite for orchestra. The little opera, too, went very well up to the appearance of Bacchus, when I began to fear that the small chamber orchestra would be inadequate for my dionysiac urges. I informed Hofmannsthal of my fears and asked him whether I could not change over at this point to 'full orchestra', if necessary

behind the stage. Admittedly a stupid idea. Hofmannsthal im-
plored me to give it up and under this benevolent compulsion
the second half has turned out to be characteristic enough in
spite of everything.

Next there followed the choice of a small theatre. The beautiful theatre in Dresden, which had already been reserved for my
first performances, seemed to me to be too large and when Max
Schillings accepted all my conditions—Reinhardt with his Berlin
ensemble, for Molière, and for the opera a cast to be chosen by
me (I was thinking of Madame Jeritza whom I had seen in
Munich in *La belle Hélène* (!!!), of the splendid tenor Jadlowker
and Frieda Hempel)—and offered me the small theatre in Stuttgart which was to be re-opened, I accepted gratefully and everything went well until the dress rehearsal. To this day I am unable
to doubt the good intentions of the Generalintendant Baron von
Putlitz and of Schillings, who was my friend; but I had not
counted on certain 'forces of destiny' which were smouldering in
the jealousy of the Stuttgart dramatic and operatic casts, because
they were only to come into action after the first performance as
a second cast, although they had been responsible for all the pre-
liminary rehearsals before the arrival of the guest artists. I had
apparently offended the producer Gerhäuser when I had replied,
somewhat rashly, to one of his technical questions: 'Reinhardt
will settle all that'.

In short, was it malice—or chance? A performance of *Undine*
had been scheduled to take place in the big theatre simultaneously with the dress rehearsal of *Ariadne* in the small theatre,
and a number of important members of the technical staff (stage
managers, etc.) whom I needed urgently had been detailed to
attend the former. In consequence everything was turned upside
down at my dress rehearsal. The painter Stern acted as stage
manager, although he had no idea of stage managing—singers
made their entrances either too late or at the wrong time, the

sets were all wrong. In short, it was a mess. I was fuming with rage and exploded in an outburst against Schillings, who was of course so innocent that I, the fool, even had to apologise after-wards to Putlitz.

The evening itself went off all right. But two things had been left out of account. Firstly, that the audience was looking forward to the Strauss opera so much that it did not show sufficient inter-est in the splendid Molière, played admirably by Reinhardt's actors, especially by the inspired Arnold, and secondly that after the Molière the amiable King Karl of Württemberg, with the best of intentions, held a reception lasting three quarters of an hour which meant that *Ariadne*, which lasts an hour and a half, began about two and a half hours after the beginning of the play, so that the audience was somewhat tired and ill-tempered. In spite of this, the result was good although the evening on the whole was too long. Thereupon the Molière was shortened more and more—apart from the inspired Pallenberg there was no actor who could have done justice to this difficult part (on which the success of the evening depended)—and in the performance of Hofmannsthal's newly-revised version of *Bourgeois gentilhomme* (to which he had added a third act) in the Deutsche Theater in Berlin the orchestra was inadequate—in short, we had no end of trouble.

The charming idea—from the most sober of prose comedies to the experience of purest music—had proved a practical failure; to express it plainly, because the play-going public has no wish to listen to opera and vice versa. The proper cultural soil for this pretty hybrid was lacking. Thus Hofmannsthal and I were forced, four years later, to undertake the operation of separating Molière and Hofmannsthal-Strauss, although the work had been successfully performed on many stages (amongst others in the Munich Residenztheater and the Berlin Schauspielhaus).

Hofmannsthal's inspired introduction, which had been cut

almost in its entirety in Stuttgart, owing to the length of the evening's programme, was composed afresh by me (and very felicitously at that, in earnest of *Intermezzo*) and thus the opera was first performed in Vienna in the autumn of 1916 with the splendid Lotte Lehmann, whom I had just discovered (and who was later to sing Ariadne, Färberin, Arabella, Octavian: an unparalleled Christine and unforgettable Marschallin) as Composer. She combined a warm voice and excellent diction with inspired acting ability and a beautiful stage appearance, all of which made her a unique interpreter of my female rôles.

The Molière play was completed by Hofmannsthal with a charming third act (with the Turkish comedy) and in this new version I incorporated parts of Lully's music which I had revised; a work whose performance, provided it was adequate in all respects, would grace any stage with opera play and ballet at its command, in company with *Egmont, Midsummer Night's Dream* and *Manfred*. But this belongs to the sad chapter: 'cultural tasks of the German operatic stage'.

Josephslegende

In the last years before the first world war the Russian ballet under its inspired leader Diaghilev, and with the incomparable Nijinsky, caused a stir in Germany as elsewhere. A guest performance in Berlin delighted me so much that I gladly took up a suggestion made by Hofmannsthal and Graf Harry Kessler that I should write something for this unique troupe, when I was shown the pantomime *Josephslegende*, the title part of which had been designed for Nijinsky. The work was first performed at the Paris Opéra on 12th May, 1914, without him, his place being taken by Massine, a weaker and not quite adequate dancer. This successful performance was followed by six further performances in Covent Garden, although anti-German feeling ran high there that June and Diaghilev, who was always in financial difficulties, did not pay me my conductor's fee (6000 gold francs) nor has he done so to this day. But it was beautiful for all that.

One of the bad habits prevalent in Paris opera was that different players played at each orchestral rehearsal, because members were allowed to send substitutes when they were giving private lessons and so prevented from attending a rehearsal. In consequence I was unable to note any progress in six orchestral rehearsals and even at the last rehearsal but one, had to reprove the first flute player for bad mistakes; he replied, that this was the first time he had been there—whereupon, of course, I became very impatient and this frightened Graf Hülsen, who happened to be present and saw the world war breaking out even then. In connection with this I would like to tell the following story: after six rehearsals Massenet once thanked the drum player during a dress rehearsal for having attended all rehearsals so far. He replied: 'Merci, maître! Mais ce soir viendra mon frère'.

When war broke out two months later we were in S. Martino de Castrozza. We succeeded with difficulty in making our way home through Austrian troop transports over the Brenner pass. When we passed Franzensfeste an Austrian officer had just had an attack of nerves and jumped from the high bridge into the river Eisack. On 1st August, the British confiscated my capital deposited in London with Edgar Speyer—the savings of thirty years. For a week I was very depressed: then I carried on with *Die Frau ohne Schatten* which I had just begun and started again from the beginning to earn money by the sweat of my brow when I had just entertained hopes of devoting myself exclusively to composition from my fiftieth year onward. *Josephslegende* was revived [1922] in Vienna, produced by Alfred Roller and the excellent ballet master Kröller. Frau Potifar: Marie Gutheil-Schoder; Joseph: Messrs. Birkmeyer and Fränzel; the wonderful costumes were by Professor Haas-Heye.

Die Frau ohne Schatten

Die Frau ohne Schatten, a child of sorrow, was completed in the midst of trouble and worries during the war when, owing to the kindness and consideration shown by a Bavarian, Major Distler, my son, whose heart had not kept pace with his rapid growth, was saved from being prematurely called up. I had already enrolled Franz as an officer cadet with the foot artillery in Mainz, but the Bavarian M.O. had the good sense to declare him unfit. These wartime worries may be responsible for a certain nervous irritation in the score, especially halfway through the third act, which was to 'explode' in melodrama.

When, in the Summer of 1918, we were staying at Aschau in the Salzkammergut with friends, Frau Nossal and the Kammer-sänger Franz Steiner (who was to become an excellent interpreter of my songs during many concert tours which took us as far as Bucharest, Stockholm, etc.), Baron Andrian called me to Vienna where, under Franz Schalk in October 1919 (sets: A. Roller, production: Wymetal) *Fr-o-Sch* was first lavishly produced with a grand cast (Kaiser: Oestvig; Kaiserin: Jeritza; Nurse: Weidt; Färberin: Lehmann; Barak: Mayr). After this first great success, its way over the German stage was fraught with misfortune. In Vienna itself, owing to the strain imposed by the vocal parts and to the difficulties over the sets, the opera had to be withdrawn more often than it was performed. At the second theatre (Dresden) it came to grief because of the imperfections of the *mise en scène* (Eva von der Osten had meanwhile ruined her voice with dramatic roles) which forced me to ask Graf Seebach after the dress rehearsal to postpone the first performance for several days. Although the orchestra under Fritz Reiner was excellent the performance suffered from the inadequate Färberin. It was a mixed pleasure.

It was a serious blunder to entrust this opera, difficult as it was to cast and produce, to medium and even small theatres immediately after the war. When, on another occasion, I saw the Stuttgart post-war production (on the cheap!) I realised that the opera would never have much success. But it has succeeded nevertheless and has made a deep impression especially in the Vienna-Salzburg performance (Krauss-Wallerstein) and finally in Munich (Krauss—Hartmann—Sievert), and music lovers in particular consider it to be my most important work.

Intermezzo

The jump into the world of romantic fairytales and the over-stimulation of my imagination by the difficult subject of *Die Frau ohne Schatten* aroused anew in me the desire to write a modern, completely realistic opera, which I had long secretly entertained, and during a week spent in Dr. Krecke's sanatorium I wrote *Intermezzo*, after I had told Hermann Bahr the story and had asked him to make a libretto of it for me. Bahr made a draft but eventually declared: 'There's only one person who can handle this story, and that's you', and so it was done. The harmless little story elicited from Max Reinhardt this praise: *Intermezzo*, he said, was so good that he could produce it as a play without altering a line. The first performance in Dresden coincided with my dismissal from Vienna.

[1942]

EDITOR'S NOTES

Page

10 A MONOGRAPH ON BEETHOVEN WOULD APPEAR TO BE BEST SUITED TO FORM THE FIRST VOLUME OF SUCH A COLLECTION: *August Göllerich, Beethoven. Die Musik, Sammlung illustrierter Einzeldarstellungen. Edited by Richard Strauss, Marquardt & Co., Berlin 1904.*

12 AVANT-GARDE: *This article is the reply to a warning manifesto by Felix Draeseke, "Die Konfusion in der Musik", printed by Karl Gruninger, Stuttgart 1906.*

23 OPEN LETTER TO A LORD MAYOR: *The letter appeared in the "Berliner Tageblatt", with the following editorial comment: "This letter is addressed by Richard Strauss to the Lord Mayor of a large city which for obvious reasons cannot be named. It will appear in the official publication of the "Deutscher Buhnenverein". The editor has made it available to us in advance, being of the opinion that the conditions with which Strauss deals might be of interest not only to this single, unnamed city, but to many other of the great cities of Germany. We are of the same opinion, and therefore we have printed it.*

44 ON CONDUCTING CLASSICAL MASTERPIECES: *The choice and arrangement has been made by the editor.*

75 ON MOZART: *Selected by the editor from various notes chosen for the "Richard Strauss number" of the "Schweizerische Musikzeitung" (June 1944). Cf. Bibliography.*

79 FRIEDRICH RÖSCH: *(Born 12 December, 1862, at Memmingen, died 29 October, 1925, in Berlin). A boyhood friend of Richard Strauss, he founded in 1898, together with Strauss and Hans Sommer, the "Genossenschaft deutscher Tonsetzer". In 1919 he was chairman of the "Allgemeiner Deutscher Musikverein".*

83 JUBILEE: *The hundredth anniversary of the Vienna Philharmonic.*

MUSICAL OFFERING: *A projected tone poem, "The Danube" which was never completed.*

91 A VALUABLE ESSAY: *Kürberger's essay is entitled "Ich möchte lesen lernen" (1848).*

103 INTERVIEW ON "DIE ÆGYPTISCHE HELENA": *Given for a Vienna broadcast. P. 104—Much annoyance before her rebirth refers to the rivalry between the Dresden and Vienna*

170

BIBLIOGRAPHY